Apocalypse on Wall Street

Apocalypse on Wall Street

David McClain

Dow-Jones Irwin
Homewood, Illinois 60430

Dow Jones-Irwin is a trademark of
Dow Jones & Company, Inc.

Acquisitions editor: Richard A. Luecke
Project editor: Joan A. Hopkins
Production manager: Stephen K. Emry
Cover Photo: Comstock Inc./Tom Grill
Compositor: Carlisle Communications, Ltd.
Typeface: 11/13 Times Roman
Printer: R. R. Donnelley & Sons Company

Library of Congress Cataloging-in-Publication Data

McClain, David, 1946–
    Apocalypse on Wall Street / David McClain.
        p.   cm.
    Includes index.
    ISBN 1-55623-115-6
    1. Stock exchange.   2. New York Stock Exchange.   3. Wall Street.
4. Program trading (Securities)   I. Title.
HG4551.M44 1988
332.64′273—dc19   88–9588

Printed in the United States of America

1 2 3 4 5 6 7 8 9 0 D 5 4 3 2 1 0 9 8

To Wendie,
who keeps these matters in perspective

PREFACE

As I looked at my calendar on the morning of Monday, October 19, the day ahead promised to be interesting but unhurried: a class in Japanese at 11 A.M. (part of my preparation for next year's sabbatical); luncheon with one of the Humphrey Fellows in residence at the University, a government official from Turkey; and an afternoon free to devote to research, if I was lucky, or to departmental affairs, if I was not.

By the time I returned from the faculty dining room and found at my office door not one but two representatives from the local electronic media, it was clear that October 19 would be both more interesting and less unhurried than I had anticipated. I remember distinctly my lack of surprise at the magnitude of the selling pressure on Wall Street. The 200-point decline in the Dow to early afternoon described by my interviewers was an historic record in absolute points and even approached the October 28, 1929 one-day percentage decline mark; but a wave of selling pressure had been foreshadowed by the turmoil in financial markets over the past days and weeks. I, like most investors, had become increasingly used to a more volatile financial environment. I made a few comments about Treasury Secretary Baker's error in allowing his dispute with German Finance Minister Stoltenberg over interest rates to break into the open. I also said that, while I sympathized with the dilemma over the dollar facing Federal Reserve Chairman Alan Greenspan, it seemed to me that his expansive and voluble comments designed to defuse inflation concerns had in fact made them worse. I then bid my interviewers farewell.

Two hours later, Miles O'Brien, a reporter from the local CBS affiliate, walked into my office. "What's your reaction to a 508-point decline?" he said. I was utterly speechless. "Think you can get your voice back by the 5:30 news?" Miles asked. "I think so," I said, and we were off to WNEV-TV's newsroom, where the chaos made scenes in the film *Broadcast News* look funereal by comparison.

Over the next two weeks, I contributed to nearly a score of newscasts, on WNEV and other stations, analyzing the most dramatic financial event to occur in more than a half century. At the same time, I discussed and dissected the market's every twist and turn with my colleagues in the Department of Finance and Economics at Boston University's School of Management and in the wider Boston academic community; with the students in my course "The Global Economy"; with old friends in finance and government in New York and Washington; and with portfolio managers from Fidelity Investments and several other Boston financial services firms, who at the time of the Crash were taking my Boston Security Analysts Society course "Using Economic Data to Make Investment Decisions." My conversations about what the Brady Commission later masterfully understated as the "Market Break" even extended to meetings of the Board of Trustees of the Acton (MA) Congregational Church. There, my good friend David Wyss, chief financial economist of Data Resources, was the chairman and I the vice-chairman.

I first began to write about the Crash, as I have done about all the important developments in the United States and international economy on a weekly basis since 1984, in the *United & Babson Investment Report* and its predecessors, published since 1919 by United Business Service, Inc., of Boston. My understanding of Wall Street has benefited enormously over these years from the nearly 75 years of accumulated market-watching wisdom of David Sargent, president of the firm, and my editor Sidney McMath. By early November, in comparing what I was saying about the Crash with what I was hearing from others, I began to consider putting my thoughts in book form. I began work on the manuscript on the day after Thanksgiving. The effort has been a challenging, but rewarding, experience, matched in intensity in my professional life only by my role in participating in the drafting of the annual

Economic Report of the President at the Council of Economic Advisers in the waning months of 1979.

I view the Crash of 1987 as a harbinger, not necessarily of depression, but most certainly of a radically different, and much more turbulent, economic and financial environment in the years to come. The meltdown analogy so widely used to characterize the market's collapse on October 19 and 20 is perhaps better than NYSE Chairman John Phelan knew when he introduced it on the afternoon of Black Monday. Just as Three Mile Island and Chernobyl showed us that we don't have all the risks of commercial nuclear power well-contained, so the Crash has demonstrated that we don't have full control yet over the new financial technology we've been using.

The increasing relevance of the computer and the growing irrelevance of the clock in global capital markets have bound the international economy more tightly together than ever before. New financial instruments and computer-based portfolio management techniques have led institutional investors to focus their trading on entire blocks of securities, with the result that they pay more attention to "market" or "economy-wide" influences rather than company or industry factors in making their investment decisions. These market factors include national economic policies in the industrial countries (that more often than not are many degrees apart) and an overhang of debt, in energy, agriculture, real estate, and in the developing world.

In this setting, the premium on international coordination of economic policies is higher than it has been since the end of the Second World War. Our ability to achieve this coordination, however, is complicated by the relative decline of the United States in the world economy and the more polycentric distribution of global economic power today. The rise of the Japanese economy and nation state, with its tradition of insularity, adds further complexity.

For now, the responsibility for coming to terms with the new financial technology devolves upon the men and women in positions of political and economic leadership in Japan, the United States, and the nations of Western Europe. In not many more years, the newly industrializing countries, China and the Soviet Union will have a greater role in these affairs. Before that occurs, however, the leaders of the West will have the opportunity to succeed or fail in the task of harmonizing their national economic objectives sufficiently to permit the global economy to realize the substantial resource allocation and economic efficiency benefits of the new financial technology.

This book offers a perspective on the prospects for quality economic leadership in the years ahead. It begins by tracing the origins of the great global bull market of the 1980s. The perspective adopted here, as throughout most of the book, is an American, Wall Street–oriented one, but substantial attention is paid to developments in London, Tokyo, and on the Continent. The growing speculative excesses of the first half of 1987 are chronicled in Chapter 2, which ends with the president's decision to appoint Alan Greenspan as the new chairman of the Federal Reserve, effective, at the beginning of August.

This change of leadership at the nation's central bank is reminiscent of a similar passing of the torch in the Federal Reserve System in 1928, when Benjamin Strong, head of the Federal Reserve Bank of New York, died. Chapter 3 provides a retrospective on Paul Volcker's contributions to the international economy during his tenure at the Fed, and discusses the similarities—and differences—between Volcker's and Strong's influences on the economies of their respective times, and the consequences (actual and expected) of their departures.

The next three chapters present a detailed account of global economic and stock market developments from August 1987 through early 1988. Greenspan's first weeks of leadership at the Fed, the proximate causes of the Crash, the workings of the new financial technology, a blow-by-blow account of the market meltdown, the attempts to pick up the pieces—all are analyzed here

Chapter 7 compares the events of 1987 with those of 1929 (and 1893, which may have more relevance), reviews the 1930 to 1933 experience in the global economy, and assays the current political and economic outlook for similarities and differences. One important and hopeful observation of Chapter 7 is that international economic relations in 1988, at least among the industrialized nations most active in the international capital markets, are able to proceed in an environment much less contaminated by war-based national animosities and resentments than was the case among the great powers in the 1929 to 1933 period.

The final chapter describes what needs to be done, both with regard to national macroeconomic policies and to financial market microstructure, in order to meet the challenges posed by the new financial technology. It concludes with the assessment that, improved over the 1930s as the climate for international economic policy coordination may be, the unpracticed character of new patterns of international economic leadership and the power of the new financial technology are such that the world economy will indeed be fortunate if it can navigate through the next several years without another "market break."

The reader of this volume will immediately recognize my intellectual debt to my mentor, the great international economist and economic historian Charles P. Kindleberger, now Professor Emeritus at M.I.T. His explanation of the Great Depression, articulated with so much style 15 years ago, has extraordinary relevance to the current international economic situation, once proper allowances are made for the remarkable new financial tools in use today.

In addition to those cited above, I have benefited particularly from discussions on various aspects of the Crash or of the current financial structure with Zvi Bodie, Alan Marcus, Donald J. Smith, and Robert Taggart, all my colleagues at Boston University. Smith, Sidney McMath, and Suzanne Lorant read substantial portions of the manuscript and offered many useful suggestions. Dr. Steven Michelson helped me learn more about the psychological dimensions of economic distress, while the Reverend Richard Olmsted added to my understanding of the religious dimensions of apocalyptic thought. None of these, of course, share any responsibility for any errors contained within.

As noted above, I have addressed some of the topics discussed herein in various forms in some of the weekly columns I have authored for the *United & Babson Investment Report* and its predecessor publication, the *United Business & Investment Report*. My thanks to United Business Service, Inc., and its wholly-owned subsidiary Babson-United Investment Advisors, Inc., for their permission to use this material.

My wife Wendie and my children have handled with uncommon love and grace the dislocations a project of such scope and intensity implies. I am more grateful to them than they know for letting me have the fun of writing this account.

Finally, I also owe a great debt to my octogenarian, retired-grain-buyer father, Stanley R. McClain, and to my late mother, V. Mabel McClain. Victims of the Great Depression themselves, they have provided the best examples of compassion for humanity and of intellectual curiosity any son could have.

For years, I responded to my father's admonition that another Crash could happen with polite skepticism. As with so many other matters, which he has had the grace not to mention, his intuition and experience have proven more useful than my intellect. It's my hope that this volume provides an optimal mixture of my contributions of all three, as applied to the Crash of 1987.

David McClain
Acton, Massachusetts
April 8, 1988

CONTENTS

CHAPTER 1

A WILD, WILD RIDE

"Can *It* Happen Again?" Every October for the last half century, business and financial journalists have opened their "tickler" files and dusted off the annual story about the 1929 Stock Market Crash and the subsequent Great Depression. Each year's article usually has had the same format: a reference to the next anniversary; followed by a review of current business conditions, with an emphasis on the similarities to 1928 and 1929; and ending with reassuring statements from leading economic authorities that a repeat of the Crash and Depression is out of the question because of fundamental changes in the structure of financial markets and the national and international economy.

October of 1987 started out the same way. Then, on October 19, *It*—or at least the first half of *It*—did, in fact, happen again. Financial markets, and the world economy, will never be the same.

APOCALYPSE AND GREED

"Black Monday," 1987, has joined the ranks of November 22, 1963, and July 20, 1969, as one of those days on which you will remember where you were while history was being made. The 508-point drop in the Dow Jones Industrial Average was off the financial Richter scale; the 22.6 percent plunge has only been rivaled by the 26 percent, two-day slide during trading on October 28 and 29, 1929.

Events of such moment and such magnitude offer us many insights about our individual and national character and consciousness. They are truly apocalyptic, or revelatory. The word *apocalypse*, from the Greek *apokalyptein*, means "to uncover." *Kalyp-*

tein in Greek means "to cover" and is part of the etymology of the word *hell*. Although stock market crashes may not contain revelations for the ages about the struggle between good and evil, they always do reveal a fundamental truth for a particular generation of investors: that making money "the old-fashioned way, by earning it," as John Housman put it in the old Smith Barney commercials, is the only sure way to accumulate lasting wealth.

That investors in every age seem to need this reminder is as much as anything a statement about the human condition; chroniclers of previous market upsets have uniformly remarked on the persistence of the tendency of investors toward speculative excess. M.I.T.'s Charles Kindleberger has characterized the subject of financial and monetary crisis as a "hardy perennial."[1] Harvard's John Kenneth Galbraith attributes investors' tendency to get carried away to "the shortness of public memory, especially when it contends with a euphoric desire to forget."[2] Yale's Burton Malkiel, in his classic *A Random Walk Down Wall Street*, sums up the phenomenon starkly: "Greed run amok has been an essential feature of every spectacular boom in history."[3] The insider trading scandals of the 1980s are no doubt only the public tip of the immense, private iceberg of desire to get very rich very quickly.

Another Gilded Age

To be sure, greed has its lieutenants in every era. In the 1920s in the United States, these included highly leveraged investment pools; an economy pushing to the forefront of the world stage at a time when the leading nation, the United Kingdom, was slipping into eclipse; minimal government regulation of markets; and a conservative, probusiness, hands-off ethic emanating from the White House.

---

[1]Charles P. Kindleberger, *Manias, Panics, and Crashes* (New York: Basic Books, 1978), p. 3.

[2]John Kenneth Galbraith, "The 1929 Parallel," *Atlantic Monthly* 259 (January 1987), p. 66.

[3]Burton G. Malkiel, *A Random Walk Down Wall Street*, 4th edition (New York: W. W. Norton & Company, 1985), p. 28.

In many respects, the 1980s resemble the '20s. Certainly, the political atmospherics are similar. Financial markets are being deregulated, in part in response to the virulent inflation of the 1970s. A veritable menagerie of new financial instruments has been created; these allow firms to hedge the risks of fluctuating interest and exchange rates, but these new instruments can be speculative vehicles. Japan is now the brash, rich kid in the world economy, and the United States is in decline. The aptly named "junk" bond and the leveraged buyout (LBO) have elevated the art of debt-financed corporate restructuring a notch. International debt problems, the legacy of the war against inflation, have overshadowed the decade, just as did the question of German reparations (for another, different kind of war) sixty years earlier.

Of Clocks and Computers

Some features are unique to the '80s, of course. The growing relevance of the computer, and the increasing irrelevance of the clock, are what's new in stock trading in this decade. Computers have allowed complicated trading strategies to be implemented much more quickly. Their use, in conjunction with the new instruments that have been developed, certainly has increased trading volume; many believe it also has added to market volatility.

Stock market trading truly has become around-the-clock and global in the 1980s, as new communications technology and the opening of the London, New York, and Tokyo exchanges to increased foreign membership have allowed nearly continuous trading of securities. As a result, the capital markets of the industrialized countries are much more tightly linked. According to one source, the communications networks of four firms supplying data to the securities markets cover more than 100,000 equities listed on more than 110 exchanges in 110 countries, and connect 300,000 terminals.[4] This capacity increases the potential for exchange rate, interest rate, and thus stock price volatility when one country's

---

[4]*Report of the Presidential Task Force on Market Mechanisms* (Washington: Government Printing Office, 1988), p. 10.

economic policies get very far out of step with another's. National governments are human institutions, so it is no surprise that this quantum jump in international economic interdependence has outstripped growth in international economic policy coordination.

Harder to Sing in Harmony

In fact, if anything, productive (as distinct from ceremonial) consultations among nations have become more difficult in the '80s, for two reasons. With the waning of the *Pax Americana* of the immediate postwar period, the global economy has become a much more polycentric environment. Not only is Japan catching up to the United States, but the "Four Tigers"—Korea, Taiwan, Hong Kong, and Singapore—also have surged to the forefront of international competition, particularly in labor-intensive products. The resulting climate of increased economic equality has made it more likely that a leadership vacuum would develop among nations, and that no country would take the lead in seeing that policies were coordinated. Ominously, this is the same development that Kindleberger identified as a principal cause of the Great Depression[5].

The Reagan Revolution, with the extraordinary sway it held over American economic policy in the first half of the decade, also has made it difficult for policy coordination to proceed smoothly. While many countries were quite sympathetic with the move to rein in government, none agreed that to approach this goal by cutting taxes without simultaneously cutting spending was sensible. The "supply-side" theory that some of the president's advisors used to dress up this radical experiment in economic policy smacked to many on the Continent and in Japan of—as George Bush had put it when running for president—"voodoo economics," and they were less than enthusiastic about falling in step with it.

Thus, the first truly global bull market—the Dow rose by 250 percent, Japan's Nikkei index by nearly 300 percent, Germany's leading barometer by almost 250 percent, Australia's by 400 percent, and the London *Financial Times* index by 250 percent—oc-

---

[5]Charles P. Kindleberger, *The World in Depression: 1929–39* (Berkeley: University of California Press, 1973), p. 28.

FIGURE 1–1
The Great Global Bull Market of the 1980s

FIGURE 1–1
(concluded)

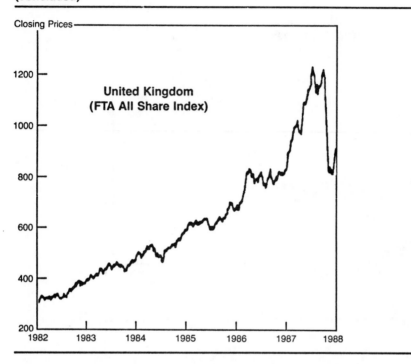

Closing Prices

United Kingdom
(FTA All Share Index)

1200

1000

800

600

400

200

1982   1983   1984   1985   1986   1987   1988

Source: *Report of the Presidential Task Force on Market Mechanisms* (Washington: Government Printing Office, 1988), pp. 10, 13.

curred against a backdrop of discordant economic policies, at a time when the premium on policy harmonization had increased sharply.

Still, markets always have to cope with risks in the fundamental economic outlook. And not all bull markets end so abruptly and catastrophically. What was it about the great global bull market of the '80s that permitted a growing role for greed and speculative excess and led to the crash of the century? How important were national economic policy considerations in the market's abrupt plunge? What was the role of the "microstructure" of financial markets—the organization of the stock and futures exchanges and their ability to handle the trading consequences of rapidly shifting investor sentiment? Finally, what can be done to prevent the Second Great Crash of the twentieth century being followed by a Second Great Depression? It is with these questions that this book is concerned.

BIRTH OF A BULL

Each market runup is unique, and to understand this one we must return to its origin. The bull market of the 1980s was born in the midsummer of 1982. Federal Reserve Chairman Paul Volcker, St. George to the dragon of inflation, had watched the fallout from his efforts—a thrift industry in crisis and the collapses of Drysdale Securities, a government bond dealer, and the Penn Square Bank in Oklahoma City—roil the financial markets. Now, in the face of the slide in oil prices that did Penn Square in, Mexico found itself unable to meet its obligations to the world's largest banks.

With the U.S. economy mired in its most severe slump since the 1930s and growth prospects in Europe and Japan still uncertain, Volcker feared a chain-reaction collapse of the debt-swollen international financial system. The Fed Chairman holstered his anti-inflation monetarist artillery and turned his attention to the bystanders wounded in the inflation fight. A bridge loan was arranged for the Mexicans while a restructuring scheme, the first of many, could be put in place; interest rates were pushed down forcefully. By year's end, the prime rate, which had stood at 16.5 percent in July, had declined to 11.5 percent.

Convinced that Volcker had made a permanent turn away from worrying about inflation toward battling unemployment and slack demand, the stock market surged. By year's end, the Dow stood at a record 1071, nearly 40 percent above the August low of 777. Abroad, lower U.S. yields meant that foreign interest rates could come down as well. (Remember, at this time the dollar was the strongest currency in the world.) Foreign markets—some of which, like that of the U.K., had been on the mend for as long as a year and a half—continued to advance in tandem with the U.S. market. So great was the available margin of excess production capacity in the global economy (i.e., so great had been the recession incurred to bring down inflation) that this one fundamental feature of the business outlook fueled expectations of greater earnings and dividends for several years into the future.

To be sure, the rise in stock market values around the world was not without its complications: The run on Continental Illinois (holder of some of those Penn Square energy loans) occurred; brinksmanship in developing country debt negotiations continued; and political tensions in the Middle East and elsewhere mounted. But the 1982 break in oil prices and continuing slow growth in Europe convinced investors that several years would pass before cost-push or demand-pull inflation could threaten the world economy, and the profits of the companies operating therein, again. It was truly a "Been Down So Long It Looks Like Up to Me"[6] situation.

Growing Pains

By the end of 1984, the strains of increased policy imbalances in a more interdependent global economy were beginning to take their toll. Though many foreign markets continued to advance, in the United States, the Dow seesawed, ending the year at 1212, 3.5 percent below the peak achieved in early January.

The bizarre U.S. fiscal policy of massive tax cuts unmatched by large expenditure reductions had been modified slightly by substantial tax increases in 1982 and 1984, but the policy was still nearly 180 degrees away from what Germany and Japan were doing (Figure 1–2). As a result of this (and a slight move toward credit restraint in the spring of 1984), U.S. real (inflation-adjusted) interest rates remained high compared to those abroad. This disparity continued to propel the dollar toward stratospheric levels, and the American Midwest became more and more economically depressed in the face of suddenly-cheaper imports and shrinking farm exports. Protectionist teachings started to enjoy a revival. Walter Mondale sought to warn the electorate about the need to harmonize our economic policy with that of other nations via a tax hike, but the election results of November 1984 revealed that the public was not yet prepared to turn its back on the seductive "politics of joy" so soon.

---

[6]From Richard Farina, *Been Down So Long It Looks Like Up to Me* (New York: Penguin Books, Inc., 1983). First published, 1966.

FIGURE 1–2
Fiscal Policy Imbalances: Cumulative Structural Government Budget Changes Since 1981

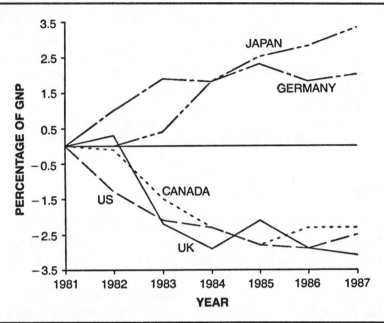

Source: Data from *OECD Economic Outlook* 39 (May 1986), p.40.

The economy's performance continued to be disappointing through the first half of 1985. Steady reductions in interest rates, accompanied by a rebasing of money supply targets that removed the spectre of a credit tightening in 1985's second half, seemed to be having little effect on economic growth in the United States. These reductions did, however, break the dollar's fever; it peaked in February. Capital spending was sluggish, and with no other country prepared to pick up the slack of weakening American spending, world trade growth was cut in half. Global stock market performance was still robust, but in the United States, most of the gains to midyear had come in a familiar January rally.[7]

---

[7]For an account of this phenomenon, see Robert A. Haugen and Joseph Lakonishok, *The Incredible January Effect* (Homewood, Ill.: Dow Jones-Irwin, 1987).

Though excess capacity remained abundant, worries about a global paralysis of economic policy and a 1930s-style deflation were beginning to make investors nervous. Just in time, the last months of 1985 brought a series of favorable developments that promised to revitalize the recovery from the severe worldwide economic slump of the early 1980s, and hence provided the basis for a further increase in share values. Oil prices fell, and an agreement was reached on a strategy for coordinating national economic policies and thereby controlling exchange-rate swings. As part of this co-ordination effort, the United States made what appeared to be meaningful strides in getting the federal budget deficit under control.

THE BULL MARKET COMES OF AGE

On September 22, 1985, finance ministers from the Group of Five (Britain, France, Germany, Japan, and the United States), met at the Plaza Hotel in New York and agreed to take steps to accelerate the decline in the dollar. This move to rebalance economic policies and exchange rates would help developing countries repay their dollar-denominated debts and would help to defuse protectionist sentiment in industrial nations. The strategy, essentially, was to rely on monetary policy, with the U.S. central bank easing more rapidly than its foreign counterparts, backed up where possible by fiscal measures.

The American obligation in the fiscal realm was well under-stood: to rein in federal budget deficits that stretched through the rest of the decade and beyond "as far as the eye can see," as David Stockman put it.[8] In a development little noticed at the time, congressional negotiators in mid-1985 had already bent the trajec-tory of military spending downward, making changes that would have the effect of reducing its 1990 level by roughly $100 billion below administration intentions. Then, in December 1985, with a mixture of fear and loathing, Congress passed the Gramm-Rudman legislation. This law put deficit reduction on automatic pilot, pro-

---

[8]See William Greider, "The Education of David Stockman," *Atlantic Monthly* 248 (December 1981).

viding that if annual targets for deficit reduction were not met by Congress according to a timetable, the comptroller general was empowered to order across-the-board reductions in spending to achieve the deficit levels specified in the law. These annual targets provided that the federal budget would be balanced by 1991.

Abroad, foreign governments were to do the opposite: spend more, or tax less. Japan complied with a 4-trillion-yen fiscal stimulus package, announced in mid-October. Characteristically, Germany was more cautious, despite an unemployment rate that remained stubbornly above 8 percent.

Oil Prices Break Downward Again

December 1985 also was the month in which world oil markets started to come apart. Saudi oil minister Sheikh Ahmed Zaki Yamani had convinced King Fahd that the Kingdom needed to reassert control over the oil market and OPEC's role in it. Since the break in oil prices in 1982, from $35 per barrel to $28, more and more OPEC members had resorted to clandestine overproduction to increase their revenues and the survivability of those in power. Saudi Arabia, ever the swing producer, had cut production to keep market prices up. Now it saw its daily pumpings slump to two million barrels per day and its daily revenues to less than $60 million. The Kingdom was being forced to draw down its assets in order to continue funding the national lifestyle it had learned to enjoy in better times.

Sheikh Yamani reasoned that the Saudis, with a production capacity of about ten million barrels per day, would be better off selling four, five, or six million barrels at a price of $18. The rest of OPEC, however, would be worse off because all the other members were already producing at levels not far from their capacity. Yamani made the argument that, if the cartel demonstrated its ability to drive prices down to a point below which production from "marginal" sources of supply (e.g., "stripper" wells in the U.S. oil patch) was not economical, these sources would have to be shut in because their owners couldn't stand the risk that the cartel would force prices down again at some time in the future. With the "competitive fringe" thus neutralized, prices could come back up, and OPEC as a whole, not just Saudi Arabia, would benefit.

The King feared reprisals from within OPEC, particularly from revenue-hungry Iran. In the end, however, he sided with Yamani's conclusion that if the Saudis did nothing, the rest of OPEC would never again take their leadership seriously. He saw in this course an even more ominous outcome for the Kingdom.

Yamani's production initiative was promoted as a new pricing scheme for Saudi crude—the "netback" method, in which prices for refined products at the time crude oil tankers arrived in port called the tune for the price of the crude delivered. The effect was to let market conditions—the balance of supply and demand—set the rate for both refined product and crude oil prices. As the Saudis opened their spigots wider and wider, oil prices tumbled below $20 and headed on down.

Favorable Atmospherics

This improvement in economic fundamentals for the West was accompanied by three less-substantive but still influential events that recast the tone of the economic outlook into more of a pro-growth vein. In mid-November of 1985, President Reagan and General Secretary Gorbachev met face-to-face for the first time in Geneva. The president nominated two new growth-oriented governors to the board of the Federal Reserve System, Treasury economist Manuel Johnson and Kansas banker Wayne Angell. Finally, at meetings of the International Monetary Fund (IMF) and World Bank in Seoul, Korea, Treasury Secretary James Baker proposed a new strategy for dealing with the worsening international debt crisis.

The original debt approach, formulated on an ad hoc basis in the months and years after Mexico's brush with default in 1982, was based on growth without protectionism in industrial countries; demand restraint (i.e., tight money and government belt-tightening) by debtors; and temporary financing by banks based on the supervision of debtor countries by the IMF. By 1985, this strategy was beginning to founder, as the strong dollar curtailed growth in the United States, economic expansion in Europe and Japan proved to be disappointing, political self-interest limited the scope of less-developed-country (LDC) actions, and commodity prices continued to be soft. The scope and duration of the crisis had clearly gone beyond the short-term, individual-country balance of payments adjustment problems the IMF was originally created to address.

The "Baker Plan" envisaged an increased flow of private bridge financing to LDCs; at the same time, the World Bank was to play a greater role in the debt workout. An increasing number of the bank's loans would be for changes in general structural policies, instead of just for projects (e.g., dams or highways), as in the past. Baker suggested that some of the private-sector loans be made in tandem with the bank and that the bank guarantee others. In return, the United States would agree to support a capital increase for the World Bank.

The Stampede Begins

Welcoming this commitment of the industrial nations to at least make a start in coordinating their economic policies, and anticipating the favorable benefits of lower oil prices, a renewed commitment to noninflationary growth, and a more orderly resolution of the international debt crisis, investors poured back into the American market and those abroad as well.

In the United States, the rally began in mid-October of 1985 as the Dow industrials posted an all-time high of 1369, breaking out of doldrums that had persisted since February after the January surge had taken the 30-stock index up 100 points from the year-end 1984 closing level. Merger activity (involving Philip Morris' takeover of General Foods) allowed the Dow to achieve the record ahead of broader market indexes. They followed in short order, however, helped by some encouraging comments about easier money from Paul Volcker (designed, no doubt, to promote a weaker dollar per the Plaza Agreement). By mid-November, the Dow had surpassed 1450, while the 30-year Treasury bond was yielding under 10 percent for the first time since 1980. At year's end, the widely watched market barometer closed at 1547, after having hit 1553 earlier in December.

Markets abroad shared in the investor euphoria, as Table 1–1 indicates. In Europe, investors shook off for the moment concerns about "Eurosclerosis"—structural rigidities that were said to hamper the competitiveness of firms in the U.K. and on the Continent. In Japan, where the Nikkei index closed at 13113, advances were more modest as stock market participants fretted about the impli-

TABLE 1–1
Global Stock Market Performance in 1985 (percent change from year-end 1984)

Country	In Local Currency	In U.S. Dollars
Australia	+40.0	+15.5
Canada	18.3	11.6
France	37.7	73.9
Germany	80.2	128.7
Hong Kong	43.7	43.8
Italy	98.5	125.9
Japan	13.1	40.4
Switzerland	57.2	95.7
United Kingdom	16.5	43.5
United States	26.4	26.4
World Index	35.6	35.6

Source: *The Wall Street Journal*, January 2, 1986.

cations of a stronger yen for economic growth. Still, when exchange rate fluctuations are taken into account, most foreign stock markets outperformed the United States market in 1985.

As 1985 ended, investors around the globe were still comforted by the fact that even in the United States, where demand expansion in the wake of the 1981-to-1982 recession had been strongest, productive capacity seemed to be ample. The Federal Reserve Board's index of capacity utilization had made up only about two thirds of the distance from the trough of the early '80s recession to its level at the preceding business cycle peak, in 1979. Outside of the United States, where multinational firms (in particular, those fleeing the high dollar) had established production facilities at an accelerated pace in low-wage countries, capacity was in even greater supply. Thus, the anticipated quickening in the pace of global spending and income was not expected to trigger another round of demand-pull inflation.

1986: BUYING ON THE BAD NEWS

One year later, stock market values again had registered new highs in nearly all the major markets, as Table 1–2 indicates, though the pace of advance was not uniform.

TABLE 1–2
Global Stock Market Performance in 1986 (percent change from year-end 1985)

Country	In Local Currency	In U.S. Dollars
Australia	+41.6	+40.4
Canada	5.7	6.9
France	52.9	78.3
Germany	5.6	32.9
Hong Kong	49.4	49.6
Italy	64.1	102.5
Japan	57.7	72.6
Switzerland	3.2	30.9
United Kingdom	19.1	21.1
United States	14.6	14.6
World Index	39.8	39.8

Source: *The Wall Street Journal,* January 2, 1987.

In the U.S. market, most of the action came in the first three months of 1986. Before the end of March, the Dow topped 1800, nearly 50 percent above the year-end 1984 level. By early July, it nosed above 1900, then drifted for several months. The *Financial Times* index peaked at over 1400 in April, then spent the rest of the year, through the City's Big Bang of stock market deregulation, pretty much in retreat, closing at 1300. In Japan, the Nikkei index staged a meteoric rise to near the 19000 mark in midsummer, suffered a 15 percent correction by early October, then regained all its lost ground by year's end.

In bidding up share prices further, investors had to shed several waves of bad news. No one item was sufficient to slow the markets' advance; indeed, the resilience of investor perceptions suggested a growing role for speculative excess. Taken together, however, these disturbing developments indicated a substantial escalation of the level of risk in the international business environment.

The Yin and Yang of Oil Prices

Almost from the beginning of 1986, it became evident that lower oil prices were something of a mixed blessing. Early in the year, prices dipped below $15, then dropped under $10 as buyers put off

purchases in anticipation of still lower prices. Small U.S. producers, who needed $15 to $20 per barrel to operate profitably, re-
trenched to satisfy their bankers. Vice President Bush made a hur-
ried trip to Saudi Arabia at the beginning of April to tell the Saudis
that lower oil prices could be too much of a good thing. OPEC's
swing producer eased off a bit, prices bobbed up to the $12-to-$13
range, long-term interest rates stabilized (at below 7½ percent for
the 30-year T bond), and the stock market paused. Bush no doubt
made the point that Mexico's interests were also ill-served by the
Saudi action, since it needed a predictable and substantial flow of
oil revenue in order to be able to roll over its debt. Certainly he
suggested that at some (very low) price of oil, Iran could become
a very desperate neighbor.

With oil prices only half the market levels of a few months
earlier and with much greater uncertainty over their future course,
energy-sector companies sharply curtailed their capital spending.
In this development lies a lesson, not widely understood at the
beginning of 1986, about the comparative impact of favorable and
unfavorable supply shocks on the economy. The 1973 to 1974 and
1979 to 1980 experiences taught us that the losers in an abrupt
escalation of oil prices (consumers of oil products) react much
faster than the winners (OPEC oil producers in other nations). That
is, we cut back our spending quickly, while the recipients of the
oil revenue windfall take a year or two to augment their spending
levels to match their increased income.

Despite this experience, most analysts expected that the winners from a fall in oil prices—this time, consumers in industrial and
non-oil-producing, developing countries—would react about as
quickly as they had when they were the losers in 1973 to 1974 and
1979 to 1980. If any significant attention was given to the losers in
industrial countries in making economic forecasts, it was focused
on Britain and Norway. These countries, along with Mexico, had
to consider OPEC's request for solidarity. Although it was understood that the oil price slump was bad news for the American
Southwest, the tenor of forecasts for the U.S. economy tended to
gloss over the problems in the oil-producing sector of the economy.

In fact, just as in the other two oil price shocks, the loser
reacted much more quickly than the winners. For the American
economy, this meant that the negative effect of reduced capital

spending in the oil patch kicked in well before the positive effect of lower heating oil and gasoline prices. As a result, economic growth in the United States in the year's first half was more sluggish than expected. Given the rather slow response of foreign governments to their pledge to stimulate demand, the U.S. weakness raised anew concerns about spiraling deflation and the resolution of the international debt crisis.

Responding to shrinking demand, central banks around the world engaged in a coordinated round of discount rate reductions in early March of 1986. This event was noteworthy because—reflecting the elevated importance of America's trading partners—the United States was not the public leader in this exercise. Paul Volcker, initially opposed to a discount rate cut, had settled for staying the hands of the new growth-oriented majority on the Fed Board, who were pushing for a reduction in mid-February. Volcker bought time to arrange a coordinated monetary policy response for demonstration to financial markets. Germany took the lead in lowering rates, followed by Japan, the United States, and several other nations. With a watchful eye on interest rate developments abroad, the Fed would cut the discount rate thrice more in 1986, in April before the early May Tokyo Economic Summit and again in July and August, in a continuing effort to restart spending and growth. Buffeted by U.S.–Libyan tensions, the Chernobyl disaster, and renewed softness in oil prices, the stock market edged higher in fits and starts.

In early August, OPEC tried to reassert its control with a new 60-day production-sharing accord, which was subsequently renewed. Late in October, perhaps concerned by new sabre-rattling by Iranians, and uncertain about American security guarantees, King Fahd sacked Sheikh Yamani and announced a return to customary forms of pricing and the more traditional Saudi role as swing producer in the cartel. At year's end, the Saudis and OPEC agreed to stabilize the price at $18 per barrel. Iraq was not an official signatory to the agreement, but its production plans were considered when the cartel set signatories' production levels.

The OPEC agreement, concluded in the final months of 1986, held up through 1987. But the calm brought to world oil markets was offset by increased political turbulence in the Middle East and by new U.S. involvement in the waters of the Persian Gulf.

Budget Disarray

In the United States, the summer of 1986 also proved to be a rocky time for the Gramm-Rudman agreement. In February, a federal court upheld a challenge to the legislation's constitutionality. The problem involved the separation of powers clause. The comptroller general's role in ordering the automatic spending reductions was the rub, since that officer was responsible to the Congress. On July 7, the Supreme Court ruled that Gramm-Rudman, as written, was unconstitutional.

Privately, members of Congress facing an election campaign in the fall breathed a sigh of relief. Publicly, they vowed to adhere to the strictures of Gramm-Rudman while working to remedy the legal problem. In practice, members of Congress found it convenient to wait until 1987 to begin serious discussions on the "son of Gramm-Rudman." In the interim, they fudged and tinkered with its targets for fiscal year 1987, embracing overoptimistic economic forecasts and counting on higher projected revenues as a substitute for tax increases and spending cuts. In the end, the other major fiscal priority for 1986, tax reform, provided a convenient windfall in revenues—a wave of capital gains realizations at the end of 1986—that permitted the legislators to put off the hard choices for another year.

Dollar Disappointment

The third pillar of the early 1986 optimism, the expected decline of the dollar, came off on schedule. By the end of the year, on a real, trade-weighted basis, the U.S. currency had fallen by about 20 percent from its February 1985 peak. (A trade-weighted exchange rate index uses export and import flows with a range of trading partner countries to measure the average change in the dollar's value against the currencies of this group of countries. A real exchange rate index adjusts market exchange rates for differences in economy-wide prices and production costs between countries.) During 1986 alone, the dollar declined in nominal terms by more than 20 percent against both the Japanese yen and the Deutsche mark.

What did not occur on time was the expected improvement in the U.S. trade account, as Americans continued their infatuation with foreign-made products. Real trade volumes did not begin to respond as expected, turning around only late in the year, and the nominal U.S. trade deficit continued to deteriorate throughout 1986. For the entire year, the red ink totaled $144 billion, 3 percent of GNP.

U.S. government officials pointed the finger of blame at foreigners, claiming they were not allowing their economies to expand rapidly enough to absorb American exports. Other analysts suggested that the problem lay in sluggish productivity growth and a gradual loss of global competitiveness in *traded* goods, not captured in conventional measures of the real exchange rate; on this interpretation, the dollar had further to fall before the trade deficit would be cured.

Foreign manufacturers were exceptionally slow to change their product prices during this phase of the dollar cycle. It's likely that these foreign producers—the beneficiaries of years of a high dollar—were now making an extra effort to hold their market share. These firms were also able to hold prices down by taking advantage of cheaper imported raw materials, the result of their stronger currencies. By the third quarter of 1986, despite the substantial fall in the U.S. currency's value, prices of goods imported into the United States were still 5 percent *below* their levels 12 months before.

The "imbalance" effect and the "J–curve" phenomenon also influenced the course of the trade deficit. The former refers to the fact that, with U.S. imports 60 percent larger than exports, exports had to rise 60 percent faster than imports just to keep the trade deficit from widening.

The *J-curve* is the name given to a graph of the path the trade balance traces over time after the depreciation of a country's currency. It tells us that after a depreciation the trade deficit gets worse before it gets better. Measured in dollars, the merchandise trade account will show a larger deficit immediately after the dollar depreciates, since as an arithmetic matter more dollars are needed to equal the price of imported goods in foreign currency. Over time, as trade volumes respond to the more competitively priced U.S. goods, export volumes should rise and import volumes decline (or rise more slowly), offsetting the initial recorded deterioration of the trade balance. Export prices should rise a bit, too. The upshot is that the trade balance response to a once-and-for-all depreciation in the dollar's value should trace out the letter *J*. In 1986, the problem was that the trade deficit was taking too long to "turn the corner" of the *J*, making investors think that the dollar might have to depreciate further.

THE POLITICAL TERRAIN GROWS
MORE UNEVEN

A final, political development capped a year that, while it will be remembered for something that looked very unlikely when it began (tax reform), failed singularly to deliver on its promise of stronger growth and an early resolution to the American "twin" (budget and trade) deficit problems. In the congressional elections held November 4, the president's party picked up eight governors' seats and lost only five seats in the House. However, the Republicans relinquished control of the Senate, as their 53 to 47 majority in the ninety-ninth Congress was transformed into a 45 to 55 minority in the one-hundredth.

This political setback for the president emphasized that the aging chief executive, at odds with the Democrats in Congress for years over the budget, now ran an even greater risk of being a lame duck. The Iran-Contra affair burst into the headlines a few days later, and the insider trading scandal aroused new suspicions about widespread abuses in our increasingly unregulated financial markets.

The stage was thus set for a more conflict-ridden 1987: conflict between the industrial nations over the correction of policy imbalances and the foreign-exchange value of the dollar; conflict between the president and Congress over the federal budget deficit (to say nothing of other issues, such as the Supreme Court and Central America); and conflict in the Middle East.

Abroad, the political landscape also was growing more unsettled. In Japan, Prime Minister Yasuhiro Nakasone had been greatly embarrassed by the public outcry against his tax reform plan. Through masterful political maneuvering, he succeeded in obtaining a one-year lease on his office, but he, too, was increasingly a lame duck, less and less able to deliver on economic policy promises to the United States. Britain and France faced the need for elections by 1988, and while Mrs. Thatcher seemed in control, the

French had labored since March of 1986 with a socialist president and a conservative national assembly and premier.

Only in Germany had Helmut Kohl's cautious leadership struck a fully responsive chord. Despite high unemployment, his Christian Democrats were expected to celebrate victory after the national elections to be held in January 1987. In its way, however, the strength of Kohl's domestic position had its dark side. It cast a pall over prospects for policy coordination among the industrial nations because it allowed his government to resist more strenuously foreign calls for fiscal reflation of the German economy.

CHAPTER 2

1987: A YEAR OF LIVING DANGEROUSLY

The political and economic problems surfacing in the closing months of 1986 argued for 1987 to be a year of, at best, consolidation in the world's equity markets. Indeed, as 1987 began, the *Economist*, deploring the flood of liquidity that had boosted share prices so strongly in 1986, intoned, "There is hardly an economy in the world as strong as its stock market."[1]

This skepticism was not shared in the least by investors. The Dow soared through the 2000 barrier in the year's first full trading week. Some observers suggested that the market's advance had been held down at year-end 1986 by selling designed to lock in capital gains at preferential tax rates. In any event, a fortnight later the Dow had pierced the 2100 threshold, bringing with it to higher ground the S&P 500, the NYSE Composite, and the AMEX. Only the NASDAQ failed to post a new mark, suggesting that stocks had been purchased in order of quality. By the end of January, the Dow was up 262 points—an excellent showing for a full year—in the space of a month.

COMING APART

Over the next several months, symptom after symptom emerged of an international economic system flirting with cardiac arrest. Asymmetric, unbalanced economic policies and worries about

---

[1]"Bulls Stampede into 1987," The *Economist* 302 (January 3, 1987), p. 55.

American inflation triggered periodic runs on the dollar, which were quickly followed by officials' increasingly *in*credible reassurances of their commitment to stable exchange rates. Stagnant industrial-country growth and the failure of the Baker initiative generated new patterns of confrontation and conflict in LDC debt negotiations. The White House played "rope-a-dope" with its critics, careening in its relations with Japan from protectionist policies one month to statesmanlike diplomacy the next. And tensions in the Iran-Iraq conflict ratcheted up several more notches. Through all of this disturbing news, the world's stock markets soared ever higher—a sign either of extraordinary confidence in the abilities of our leaders to address the worsening crisis or of the spreading infection of speculative fever. Lending weight to the latter interpretation was an increase in market volatility.

The Dollar Takes a Hit

Bullish sentiment was fueled by those analysts who found justification for the market's quick runup in economic fundamentals. Tax reform had been widely expected to pull demand from 1987's first half into the final months of 1986, leaving an "air pocket" of demand—which investors expected to be accompanied by lower interest rates. Further, traditional indicators of future production and income levels, such as the monthly survey of the National Association of Purchasing Management, continued to advance. Consumers' confidence was rising sharply, pyramiding sentiment on sentiment.

The expectations of lower interest rates, however, also translated into renewed pressure on the dollar. By January 19, the U.S. currency had lost 10 percent of its value of 30 days earlier against the mark, dropping to 1.80 marks per dollar, and at 150 yen to the dollar was off 8 percent. By month's end, the Bundesbank had lowered its discount rate half a point, to 3 percent, as Helmut Kohl's coalition with the more centrist Free Democrats was returned to office.

This German support for the dollar was essential, since the president's budget had been declared "dead on arrival" and his State of the Union message on January 27 had not succeeded in dispelling concern over the widening Iran-Contra affair. Further complicating matters were Treasury Secretary Baker's intimations that the dollar might need to go lower, which contrasted with Fed Chairman Volcker's insistence that a substantial further fall risked inflation. By February 20, however, when the central bank head presented the Fed's annual report to Congress, the two were again on the same wavelength—giving Volcker more freedom to inform his audience that the Fed was abandoning its target for the narrowly defined money supply, M1 (essentially, currency plus checkable deposits), which had grown at double-digit rates during 1986.

Ongoing shifts in the demand for interest-bearing checking accounts, mirrored in abrupt changes in the opposite direction in the velocity or rate of turnover of M1, were responsible for the Fed's decision. These shifts were both difficult to predict and, as investment balances and not transactions vehicles, less relevant to the conduct of monetary policy anyway. In this session, Volcker responded to a query about whether he would accept reappointment to a third term as Federal Reserve Chairman (his second term was to expire August 5, 1987) with the words, "I don't think I want to comment on that question."[2]

Volcker's stature was a bulwark against the blizzard of bad news that hit the wires earlier in February. Inflation at the producer level was up sharply; rising energy costs, reflecting OPEC's new-found solidarity, were the culprits. Consumer confidence, having risen by 4 points to 94, slumped to 86. The dollar was hovering just above its mid-January lows, but frequent, strategic central bank support was suspected. The Tower Commission report was about to see the light of day, and White House Chief of Staff Donald Regan and the president's wife were at odds over everything from the chief executive's postprostate surgery schedule to Regan's handling of the Iran-Contra affair.

Brazilian Brinksmanship and the Louvre Accord

Against this background, Brazil's central bank governor resigned in a policy dispute with the country's finance minister, Dilson Fu-

---

[2]Quoted in The *Economist* 302 (February 21, 1987), p. 23.

naro, over whether interest rates should be free to reflect the country's latest takeoff into hyperinflation. In mid-1986, two-month certificates of deposit were yielding 20 to 25 percent; by early February, the rate was up to nearly 800 percent. Shortly thereafter (on the same day that Volcker was testifying before Congress), with Brazil's foreign exchange reserves depleted to less than half of their level 12 months earlier, Brazil's President Sarney announced the suspension of interest payments on $68 billion of commercial bank debt, representing about two-thirds of total Brazilian obligations to foreigners.

The Sarney decision represented the failure of the much-heralded Cruzado Plan, implemented in early 1986, in which a currency reform was combined with a tough price freeze to rein in the country's triple-digit inflation. Early results were favorable, but the populace, weary from a half-decade of austerity programs, went on an elaborate and broad-based spending spree. When price controls were lifted to address the growing problems of shortages, Brazil was sucked into hyperinflation once again.

Two days later, on February 22, heads of the major industrial nations meeting in Paris sought to defuse one source of risk in the global economy, that of gyrating currency values. The connection to the Brazilian debt repudiation was implicit but obvious: Other indebted nations had to be given an incentive to continue to pay interest. A stable dollar, and consequently stable U.S. interest rates—to which their floating-rate loans were tied—would make it easier for Mexico, Argentina, Venezuela, and other nations to continue with debt rescheduling programs. The Louvre Accord promised the stability desired and also included the usual pledges from both sides of the Atlantic and from Japan to make the necessary macroeconomic policy changes to permit exchange rates obtaining in mid-February to be equilibrium rates. Indeed, just before the Paris parlay, the Bank of Japan lowered its discount rate one-half point, to 2.5 percent.

Four days after the Accord, Mr. Funaro started touring the capitals and financial centers of the industrialized world promoting his idea of a new "grand design" to replace the case-by-case approach to the LDC debt crisis that had prevailed since Mexico first coughed in 1982. Funaro's strategy would eclipse the much-hated IMF with the friendlier World Bank as the source of multilateral funds; lower spreads and cap interest payments at a fraction, say 2.5 percent, of a country's GNP to ensure the availability of sufficient resources to promote growth in debtor nations; and introduce various schemes to convert debt into other types of assets (equity, World Bank-backed bonds, and the like). These proposals would have forced creditor nations to shoulder more of the burden of adjustment to the debt overhang. They signaled the entrance into a new, more confrontational and thus more dangerous phase of the debt minuet. Indeed, in the wake of the Funaro bombshell, bankers, prodded a bit by Paul Volcker, rushed to close rescheduling agreements with Chile and Venezuela—at reduced spreads over LIBOR (the London Interbank Offer Rate, a barometer of the banks' cost of funds). The U.S. government, for its part, advanced Argentina a bridge loan of $500 million to facilitate its reentry into new debt negotiations. And work on a rescheduling pact for Mexico was accelerated.

A MORE VOLATILE MARKET FORGES AHEAD

As if this weren't enough action for the financial markets to swallow, February also saw more insider trading arrests, conducted on site at Kidder Peabody, as well as the beginning of debate on Senate and House bills designed to put more (protectionist?) teeth in the nation's trade laws. Still high on the joyride, however, the Dow edged briefly over the 2200 mark during the month's first week, paused for a rest, then surged another 54 points (at the time, a daily record) on February 17. By month's end, despite the accumulated bad news from Brazil and the Tower Commission, the popular market index had retreated only 0.5 percent, to 2224.

The February 17 jump was the latest in a series of sharp daily moves that began to attract the attention of the Securities and Exchange Commission. During the trading of January 23, the Dow had dropped 115 points in one hour during the afternoon, after rising 64 points earlier in the day. And on September 11, 1986, the Dow had plunged 110 points intraday, finishing down 87 points from the previous close. Investors had become familiar with the problem of the "triple witching hour," the phenomenon that occurred four times a year when the stock index futures contract, options on the index, and options on individual stocks expired simultaneously. Regulators had taken steps to introduce a more orderly process into the settlement of these three types of instruments by requiring market-on-close orders to be queued at 3:30 instead of 4:00 P.M. (later, in June, they further defused the triple witching hour by going to a market-on-open settlement system for the S&P 500 index futures contract). But these sharp price moves of September 11, January 23, and February 17 occurred on days when the witches were at home. In response to the January 23 downdraft, the Chicago Mercantile Exchange raised the margin requirement for an S&P 500 futures contract to $10,000 from $6,000; the market value of the S&P 500 basket at the time was about $130,000.

The market advanced further during March's first week, impressed with the president's mea culpa in response to the Tower Report as well as with General Motors' announcement that it intended to buy back 20 percent of its common stock over the next several years. The shakeup at the National Security Council under its new director, Frank Carlucci, and the appointment of Howard Baker as the new White House chief of staff seemed to assure investors that the president was back in the saddle. The latest purchasing managers' survey suggested that the expansion was intact, and the Dow rocketed to another new high, 2280. In the following week, the S&P 500 and the NYSE Composite joined the Dow, reaching record plateaus of their own.

A Whiff of Protection—And the Prime Turns Up

So enticing, and yet so dangerous. While market letters expressed amazement at—and enthusiasm for—the incredible buoyancy of securities prices, the overvalued dollar and the mountain of increasing LDC debt continued to work their debilitating effects on credit markets. At the end of March, they would trigger the release of the first dose of a deadly poison to stocks: rising interest rates. Not every uptick in bond yields does the market in, of course, but a good case can be made that the last days of 1987's first quarter saw the beginning of the end of the great global bull market of the '80s.

In the subsequent fortnight, however, there was little evidence of the dynamics that were bringing the market to a turning point. The Dow blasted through a triple witching hour, to 2334, as investors were cheered by a chorus of good economic news: healthy fourth-quarter 1986 profits, booming housing starts and building permits, a rebound in orders, and a pullback in inflation.

In the following week, the market took off for 2400, but faltered. On March 27, the Reagan administration (looking for an opportunity to "stand tall" again?) moved to penalize Japan for violating, in sales to third-party countries, a semiconductor pricing agreement reached in 1986. The White House announced that it would impose $300 million worth of tariffs on Japanese goods, with the exact list of products to be decided by mid-April. Spooked by this whiff of protectionism, the Dow lost 94 points on that day and Monday, March 30.

Then, on March 31, Citibank made the fateful move: It boosted its prime rate from 7.5 percent to 7.75 percent. Some said this was an opportunistic hike, designed less to reflect market conditions than to restore profit margins in the wake of Brazil's interest moratorium. But long term bonds also reacted, as 30-year Treasury yields climbed to 7.9 percent from 7.55 percent a week earlier.

Another Dollar Debacle

The bond market's nervousness, which had contributed to the Citibank move, was the product of a two-week slide in the dollar's value against the yen, a slide that central bank intervention had had no luck in arresting. Sabre-rattling by U.S. Trade Representative Clayton Yeutter in advance of the semiconductor decision bore some of the blame; mixed signals from the Treasury and the Fed shouldered the rest. Treasury Secretary Baker was reported to have said that the U.S. had "no particular" rate in mind for the dollar. When Fed Chairman Volcker expressed again his concern that a falling dollar would rekindle inflation, investors lost no time in building higher expectations of inflation into bond yields.

For a moment, the market seemed ready to focus on the favorable side of a weaker dollar: stronger profits. Or perhaps the impetus was simply the fact that March 31 was the end of the Japanese fiscal year and certain Japanese financial institutions were allowed to increase their foreign holdings effective April 1. In any event, after closing the quarter at 2305, the Dow zipped up to 2390 by week's end, and on Monday, April 6, topped the 2400 barrier, closing at 2406. Across the Pacific, Japan also seemed surprisingly unconcerned about protectionist sentiment in the United States, as the Nikkei index continued its pattern of new highs as well. Its close of 22875 on April 7 was 52 percent up from a year earlier.

As the second week of April wore on, however, and the long Treasury bond's yield edged above 8 percent for the first time in 13 months, the stock market could no longer ignore the bad news and began to slip back. In mid-week, finance ministers from the Group of Seven (the Group of Five plus Canada and Italy) met in Washington to discuss the dollar's decline, but without any apparent effect. The U.S. currency slumped a further 4 percent against the yen in the four days after the Washington gathering, to 140.5 yen/dollar. As it did so, prices of 30-year Treasuries fell in concert, producing a yield of 8.6 percent by April 14—a full one percentage point rise in little more than two weeks. The merchandise trade deficit numbers for February, released that day, didn't help either, showing a worse-than-expected deterioration, to −$15.1 billion.

The problem with the G–7 meeting was that no new monetary or fiscal policy initiatives accompanied it. Both the Japanese and German central banks, with discount rates already at postwar lows, were reluctant to reduce them further. The Japanese did show up with yet another package of stimulative fiscal measures, but like their predecessors, these failed to impress. Worse, the Germans, despite experiencing a sharp slowdown in growth, refused to commit themselves to any fiscal expansion of demand at all.

As a result, the dollar continued to slump against the mark and the yen through the remainder of April, dipping below 140 yen and 1.80 marks on April 24. By then, the Dow had given up about 7 percent of ground from its early-April peak. The market correction was characterized by substantial volatility, with days of near-record increases followed by huge declines.

Concern over the rising yen threw a scare into the Tokyo market, too. On April 27, the Nikkei index lost 831 points, a record in absolute (though not percentage) terms. The following day, the market dropped another 1066 points, until widespread buying by the major Japanese securities houses reduced the decline at the close to 183 points. Through April 28, the Japanese market barometer had lost over 4 percent from its peak of 24098.

Nakasone to the Rescue

Intending to head off the risks of financial disaster and a trade war, Japan's Prime Minister Nakasone paid an urgent visit to Washington. The day before he arrived, a belligerent House of Representatives passed a trade bill containing the Gephardt Amendment, which would mandate retaliatory steps against nations that did not cut their trade surpluses with the United States. Despite this inhospitable welcome, the Japanese leader's return home was shortly followed by significant Japanese participation in the $29 billion, 30-year U.S. Treasury bond offering on May 7, thereby stabilizing bond prices, which had fallen by 12 percent since late March. Six days later, all of the major financial and industrial firms in Japan were summoned to either the Ministry of Finance or the Ministry of International Trade and Industry and told to stop "excessive speculation" against the dollar.

This help from abroad, whether cosmetic or substantive, was not enough to lift the market out of its doldrums for very long. Concern over U.S. real growth quickening too fast, commodity prices rising too swiftly, the anticipated pass-through in production costs from a weaker dollar, the Fed's nudging short-term rates up ever so slightly, another quarter-point rise in the prime rate (to 8 percent)—all combined to keep the market moving sideways, albeit in its now-customary yo-yo fashion. The beginning of the televised Iran-Contra hearings didn't help leadership concerns, either.

Abroad, Tokyo resumed its explosive upward momentum for a time and London reacted favorably to Mrs. Thatcher's decision to call a general election for June 11. But in the three days ending on May 20, the Japanese market suffered a violent correction, as the Nikkei index lost over 5 percent of its value

CITICORP RAISES THE ANTE

Into these already turbulent markets came a grenade tossed by Citicorp's chairman, John Reed. After the Tokyo market closed on May 20, the bank announced an increase in its reserves of $3 billion to reflect possible losses on its $12 billion LDC debt portfolio, bringing its total reserves to $5 billion. German and Swiss banks had been building loan-loss reserves for some time, but their U.S., British, and Japanese counterparts had been much slower to act. The deteriorating global economic outlook had pushed loan-loss reserves from just under 50 percent as a percent of nonperforming assets at the end of 1986 at many American institutions to only one-quarter to one-third three months later. Brazil's suspension of interest payments on most of its mountain of foreign debt was, of course, the cause. Table 2–1 details the foreign debt exposure of Citibank, its American competitors, and other multinational banks, as of early 1987.

Three factors had led to Brazil's suspension, and they contributed in like manner to Citibank's response. Real growth in industrial nations, particularly outside the United States, was stagnating, and so were the markets for LDC exports. The Baker Plan, so widely heralded at its unveiling in September 1985, had proven a nonstarter as a path to consensus among creditors and debtors for a more "permanent" approach to loan workouts. Finally, the dollar's decline had boosted U.S. interest rates and debt-servicing costs for LDC borrowers.

Dilson Funaro's response had been to take a harder line against the commercial banks. But when, by late April, he had failed to win new concessions quickly enough to yield political benefits for the Sarney government in Brazil, he was sacked.

John Reed also sought a more confrontational response, and a new approach, to the worsening situation. By admitting that many of the loans on his books were not worth the values accountants had placed on them, he intended to remove a weapon from the debtor countries' negotiating arsenal—and to pave the way for more sweeping measures, such as outright loan sales and debt-for-debt and debt-for-equity swaps, at the discounted market prices currently prevailing in the thin secondary market.

Wall Street acknowledged the wisdom of the Citicorp chairman's admission that the emperor had no clothes by bidding his firm's shares up 6 percent on May 21. But while realism has its virtues, it is not without risks. Not all creditors were in the strong financial position of Citibank. Still, for appearances' sake, even the weakest would have little choice but to make a nominal addition to loan-loss reserves. Differential financial conditions also made it

TABLE 2–1
Latin Debt Exposure of Major Banks at Time of Citicorp Announcement

Banks	Loans Outstanding ($ billions)	Loans as a Percentage of Equity	Reserves as a Percentage of Exposure (*)
United States			
Citicorp	11.6	80	25
Bank of America	7.3	178	29
Chase Manhattan	7.0	190	15
Morgan Guaranty	4.6	88	20
Chemical Bank	5.3	168	20
Manufacturers Hanover	7.6	202	13
United Kingdom			
Barclays	4.0	65	7
Lloyds	8.7	193	7
Midland	7.1	210	8
National Westminster	4.2	54	13
Japan (**)			
Bank of Tokyo	5.2	128	>5
Dai-Ichi Kangyo	3.4	57	>5
Fuji Bank	2.6	41	>5
Industrial Bank of Japan	2.6	58	>5
Germany (**)			
Deutsche Bank	3.4	40	70
Commerzbank	3.2	115	na
Dresdner Bank	3.4	na	50
Switzerland (**)			
Credit Suisse	1.6	39	>30
Swiss Bank Corporation	2.1	35	>30
Union Bank of Switzerland	2.4	40	>30

(*) For U.S. and U.K., Latin American exposure only; for other countries, exposure to 31 developing nations.
(**) Loans to 31 developing countries.
na = not available.

Source: The *Economist* 303 (May 30, 1987), p. 75. Reprinted with permission.

likely that creditor banks would have difficulty in presenting a united front in debt negotiations—and that creditor nation governments and central banks would have to be more alert to the possibility of runs on weaker banks.

Despite these concerns, by early June Chase Manhattan, Security Pacific, the Bank of Boston, and even the beleaguered Bank of America all had made additions to their loan-loss reserves. In midmonth, the Manufacturers Hanover joined in, as did Bankers Trust. National Westminster was the first British bank to follow suit, on June 16. The Japanese strategy, at least in the case of their Mexican exposure, was to write it down to secondary-market levels, then put it on the balance sheet of a jointly owned Cayman Islands company.

The Dollar Revives

Wall Street's reaction during the last ten days of May to John Reed's dose of *realekonomik* was to take it, as well as the attack (apparently inadvertent) by Iraq on the *Stark* and the administration's decision to reflag Kuwaiti tankers, in stride. The market was more impressed by the stabilization of the dollar, which bobbed up to be worth more than 140 yen and 1.8 marks. Contributing factors to the U.S. currency's surprising rebirth were good news releases on trade and on foreign interest rates, particularly at the long end of the spectrum. In mid-May, the March merchandise trade deficit was reported to be $13.6 billion, down from February's $15.1 billion in red ink; a 13 percent jump in exports led the way. The 30-year Treasury bond yield, which had floated up to near 9 percent, was now nearly 5.5 percent above the Japanese government long bond and almost 3 percent higher than the German. Both foreign yields had declined in part because their appreciating currencies had made inflation less of a risk. The late-May yield differentials were 1 percent wider than those that had obtained for most of the spring.

Encouraged that foreign investors, particularly the Japanese, might interpret the dollar's newfound strength as evidence of a longer-term trend of stabilization, and thus of the elimination of the risk of capital losses on their U.S. equity investments, the market poked its nose above 2300 on the strength of a 55-point post–Memorial Day holiday session, then ended the week and the

FIGURE 2–1
The Dow during the First Five Months of 1987

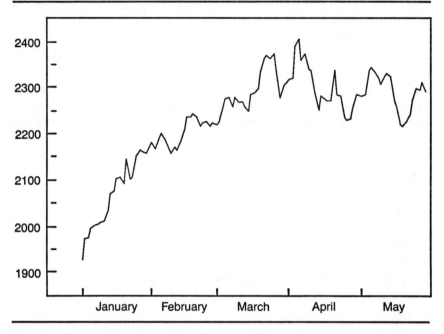

Source: United Business Service, Inc.

month at 2291. In five months, the latest leg of the Dow's wild ride had put it 400 points, or 21 percent, above year-end 1986 levels. Foreign markets typically had even bettered the U.S. performance; in Britain the *Financial Times* index was up 28 percent, while in Japan the Nikkei barometer had risen 31 percent since December 31. Germany was the odd man out, showing a decline of 15 percent, the result of concerns over sputtering growth and the impact of the appreciating mark.

In hindsight, it is easy to find in the first five months of 1987 all the early warning signs of a dangerously unstable market environment: currency unrest fed by policy conflicts, a debt interest moratorium and a confrontational response, protectionism, rising interest rates, and larger and larger swings in stock prices.

Despite the turbulence, several market gurus thought the rally still had a long way to go, and they had plenty of followers. Robert

Prechter, Elliott-wave disciple whose investment newsletter's subscription list had grown from 3,000 to 15,000 in 1986, saw the Dow topping out slightly above 3500 sometime in 1988. When pressed, Prechter would reveal his outlook for the period after the peak: A plunge in the Dow to below 1000 and a depression worse than that of the 1930s.[3]

At May's end, the Reagan administration had a more pragmatic, less cosmic focus: whether or not to reappoint Paul Volcker as the Fed Chairman for another four-year term. The Venice Economic Summit was to begin June 8, and at such a forum, speculation would naturally be rife, since Volcker's second term was to conclude two months later. In the much more volatile market environment of 1987, Volcker's stature would be a distinct asset. Still, with an election less than 18 months away, the Republican Party—and the president—certainly might be better off with someone with a less independent turn of mind.

---

[3]Reported in The *Economist* 303 (April 18, 1987), p. 13.

CHAPTER 3

THE PASSING OF A LEGEND

On June 2, 1987, the President announced that Paul Volcker had "decided against" a third four-year term as chairman of the Federal Reserve Board. Washington and Wall Street insiders saw it differently: Frustrated by the unsolved problems that still bedeviled the international financial system, Volcker had wanted to stay on, *if* he could have the president's unequivocal support. Instead, the president turned to Alan Greenspan, former head of President Ford's Council of Economic Advisers, an informal advisor to the Reagan administration, and a respected private forecaster. Bond prices experienced their largest one-day reversal in five years, the dollar fell and required central bank support, and the stock market's momentum was arrested. The day's events were a measure of the man.

WARMING UP FOR DESTINY

Paul Volcker dominated the stage of the world economy during the 1980s. To understand the way he interpreted his role in this decade, we must look to his career in earlier periods. Volcker took his undergraduate degree at Princeton and did graduate work at Harvard and the London School of Economics. He alternated between positions at the Chase Manhattan Bank and the U.S. Treasury from the late 1950s onward, until he emerged as the Undersecretary of the Treasury for Monetary Affairs during the Nixon administration. In this capacity, he made his international reputation, serving as front man with European central bankers for Treasury Secretary John Connally when the United States suspended the external convertibility of the dollar into gold in August 1971. Subsequently, he represented the administration in negotiations over the exchange rates in that December's Smithsonian Agreement, the subject of Richard Nixon's famous, hyperbolic line, "the greatest monetary agreement in the history of the world." Two years later, with the Smithsonian accord breaking apart, he was the global point man for then-Treasury Secretary George Schultz.

The Dollar Crisis of 1978

After President Nixon resigned, Volcker spent a brief period at Princeton's Woodrow Wilson School of Public and International Affairs, then was tapped to head the Federal Reserve Bank of New York. In that capacity, during the Carter administration he increasingly came into conflict with G. William Miller, the former Textron executive selected by President Carter to replace the venerable Arthur Burns as Federal Reserve chief. Miller and Treasury Secretary Michael Blumenthal had combined easy money and some rather free-wheeling comments about "benign neglect" to precipitate a dollar crisis in 1978.

His international experience told Volcker that the financial markets and foreign governments expected a more circumspect tone and more assertive action from American officials regarding the dollar's value. Though dollar declines were almost always self-correcting in theory and usually in practice, Volcker knew that exchange markets, like all financial asset markets, tend to overshoot long-run equilibrium values, and that politicians—and corporate treasurers—can spend a long time in the wilderness waiting for vicious cycles (of depreciation, inflation, and depreciation) to turn into virtuous ones.

Further, with the global economy recovering from one oil shock and fearing another, Volcker was aware that a runaway decline in the dollar's value would tempt OPEC to price its oil in a basket of currencies, abandoning the exclusive use of the dollar. Perhaps more than most, the New York Fed Chairman appreciated the unique advantage the United States possessed as the supplier of dollars—the language of international commerce—to the world economy. Like any sovereign with a monopoly on the currency printing press, the United States was able, by the simple fact that its currency was used as a means of payment in transactions between all nations (and in transactions within more than a few), to acquire resources in a way in which other nations could not.

As 1978 wore on and inflation accelerated in the overheated U.S. economy, the Fed had responded with what was to Volcker an inadequate series of discount rate hikes. President Carter had then tried to hold inflation expectations in check with a half-baked "real wage insurance" plan. The scheme, which had not been fully analyzed by his staff when the president went public with it, promised compensation via the income tax system to those who held their wage increases down in the face of rising inflation. Financial markets immediately realized that real wage insurance represented an open-ended claim on federal tax revenues should inflation get out of control for any reason other than rising wages.

With the dollar's decline turning into a rout, the Carter administration finally arranged a rescue effort that vindicated Volcker's concern with external perceptions about the prudence and assertiveness with which monetary policy had been conducted. The most striking feature of the rescue effort was the issuing of $10 billion in foreign currency government bonds, to be sold exclusively in Germany and Switzerland. In effect, to rescue the dollar the American government had been forced, like a developing country, to issue liabilities in foreign investors' currency. In Volcker's mind, this embarrassment could have been avoided with less loose talk about the dollar and a firmer hand on the monetary rudder.

A Second Oil Shock

The crisis passed, and the dollar stabilized, but only for a short while. As 1979 unfolded, the fall of the Shah of Iran coincided with a second massive rise in oil prices and prospects of another dramatic transfer of income to OPEC.

Carter administration policymakers were acutely aware that the tripling of oil prices in 1979 represented, in dollar terms as a fraction of GNP, a greater shock than the 1974 episode, and they feared another recession worse than the last. From his New York vantage point, however, Paul Volcker knew that the expectations of inflation coming into the shock in 1979 were much worse than they had been in 1974. Then, the "underlying" rate of inflation—

the trend rate of increase of prices and costs, stripped of any transitory influences—was still about 5 percent.

In contrast, this underlying rate in early 1979 was probably closer to 8 or 9 percent. As a result, consumers were steeped in a buy-in-advance mentality that would serve to keep the economy afloat in the first months after the second oil shock. Volcker read the dangers to the economy and to the international payments system—perhaps incorrectly—as coming more from an America perched on the threshold of hyperinflation rather than from the world's largest producer about to stumble into a deep recession.

In from the Bullpen

On July 15, in his much-maligned "malaise" speech, President Carter identified the root of the nation's problems in a crisis of spirit. Financial markets judged otherwise, and still unconvinced of the administration's resolve concerning inflation, boosted short-term yields by one-half of a percentage point. As part of a Cabinet reshuffle designed to demonstrate that he was indeed coping effectively with the inflation generated by the oil crisis and with the dollar, which was heading back toward its 1978 lows, President Carter brought William Miller over from the Federal Reserve to head the Treasury Department in place of the resigning Blumenthal. Tony Solomon, then Undersecretary of the Treasury for Monetary Affairs, recommended to the president Paul Volcker as Miller's replacement. Jimmy Carter is reported to have said "Who's Volcker?" and to have sounded out Bank of America CEO A. W. Clausen about the Fed's top spot. When Clausen declined, Carter chose Volcker.[1,2] Six months later, the president had come to know who Paul Volcker was—and what he stood for—all too well.

Volcker believed that the again-runaway dollar could only be corralled by bringing American inflation down. Upon taking over at the Fed in August, he pushed through a one-half point discount rate increase with the unanimous support of the seven-member

---

[1]Reported in *The Economist* 303 (May 30, 1987), p. 20.

[2]William Greider, "Annals of Finance (the Fed)—Part I," The *New Yorker* (November 9, 1987), p. 75, is the source for the Clausen vignette.

Board of Governors. One month later, however, when the rate was raised again by half a point, the board was divided and approved the second increase only by a vote of four to three. While impressed with Volcker's position, the markets were upset about the division of opinion on the board, and the dollar declined further.

At the annual meetings of the International Monetary Fund, held that year in Belgrade, Yugoslavia, the Federal Reserve chairman was stunned by the lack of confidence in American policymakers. Central bankers and political leaders from other industrial nations, particularly Germany, expressed a distinct unwillingness for a second round of dramatic dollar support measures. Reflecting the consensus in the economics profession that in the long run inflation was largely a monetary phenomenon, they spared no energy in castigating the Federal Reserve for pursuing a gradualist approach to slowing inflation's momentum and for consistently overshooting its money supply targets.

The Federal Reserve had begun announcing its targets for money supply growth at congressional insistence in 1975. The markets, and the Fed, had placed greatest emphasis on the central bank's target for M1. But in its day-to-day operations, the Federal Reserve Open Market Desk in New York had focused on the Federal funds rate—the rate banks charge each other for borrowing and lending the deposits they hold with the Fed (i.e., their reserves).

(The Fed controls the supply of these reserves directly via open market operations—purchases and sales of government securities—and indirectly via the level of its discount rate, the rate at which banks can borrow more reserves if they need them. The volume of bank reserves available affects the amount of loans banks can make and thus their deposit base, part of the money supply. Hence, when the Fed added or drained reserves to hit a particular Federal funds target, this action had a side-effect on the money supply. In other words, the Fed could focus on an interest rate target and take the consequences on the money supply; or it could focus on a money supply target and take the consequences for interest rates. It could not do both. In the late 1970s, the Fed pursued interest rate targets that required the provision of more reserves than were consistent with its money supply targets; as a result, it consistently overshot them.)

THE MOMENTOUS SWITCH TO MONETARISM

Paul Volcker returned to Washington before the Belgrade meeting ended. He had informed administration officials en route to Belgrade that he had asked a few senior Fed staffers to analyze the consequences of abandoning the traditional practice of interest rate targeting and replacing it with the management of bank reserves to ensure that the Fed's money supply targets were hit. Administration economists at first recoiled from the idea as had several Fed governors; they knew that, in the late-1979 environment of strong economic demands, weaning the economy from its dependence on a generous flow of money and credit in such a "cold turkey" fashion would mean higher interest rates and would likely bring on a recession in an election year.

His views having been confirmed by the European trip, however, Volcker persisted in his intention to shock the financial markets with this demonstration of the Fed's inflation-fighting resolve; by some reports, he had to threaten to resign to win the board's backing. On Saturday, October 6, the day the policy change was approved by the Federal Reserve Open Market Committee and announced, the president gave public support to Volcker's historic decision and an increase in the discount rate to 12 percent. Administration officials later suggested that the president's only other option was to conduct a strident, populist, anti-high interest rate campaign against the Fed—a stance that would have weakened the dollar even further and one that Jimmy Carter opposed on practical grounds: He couldn't repudiate the man he had just appointed.[3] Word of the policy change eclipsed even Pope John Paul II's visit in U.S. news coverage.

To implement this policy, the Fed widened the "bands" within which it instructed the Open Market Desk to allow the Federal funds rate to trade, from 50 basis points (one-half of a percentage point) to 400. As Figure 3–1 shows, the worst fears of Carter's economic advisors were fulfilled. The Federal funds rate topped 15 percent in the fourth quarter of 1979 and then reached nearly 20

---

[3]Ibid., p. 112.

FIGURE 3–1
The Impact on Interest Rates of the Fed's Switch to Monetarism

Percent per year, Federal Funds Rate

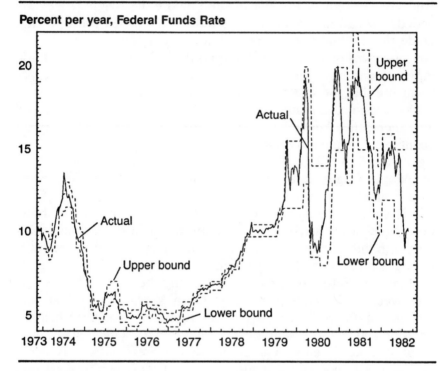

Source: Ralph C. Bryant, *Controlling Money: The Federal Reserve and Its Critics* (Washington: Brookings Institution, 1983), p. 96.

percent in early 1980, as the Fed succeeded in bringing money growth to heel. During this time, long bond rates also rose sharply, by over 3 percentage points, forcing huge capital losses onto bond underwriters and bond holders. (A widely followed, $1 billion IBM bond issue in October was worth only $790 million four months later; interestingly, among underwriters Salomon Brothers is reported to have limited its losses substantially by using a relatively new financial product, the Treasury bond futures market.)

Recession, Recession

Over the next two and one-half years under Paul Volcker's leadership, the Fed adhered to its monetarist intentions, at least in public. Interest rates gyrated violently, dropping in the short, sharp recession that ensued when credit controls were imposed in the spring of 1980, bouncing back with the economy when they were lifted, and fluctuating in a range between 13 and 20 percent during the first 20 months of the Reagan administration. The delayed impact of the oil shock and high real interest rates abetted by the Fed's attempts to ratchet money growth downward finally forced the economy into a second recession in mid-1981.

The first installment of the individual and corporate tax cuts legislated as part of the Economic Recovery Tax Act went into effect in October of that year, and the second phase kicked in the following July. Yet, in the summer of 1982, the economy was still in recession—the worst it had experienced since the 1930s. Volcker had wanted to wring inflation out of the system, but observers wondered if he had expected the cost to be that high.

Monetarism's Achilles' Heel

In fact, and quite ironically, at the very moment the Fed chairman embraced the tenets of monetarism—a school of thought that had been growing in influence for 15 years and whose intellectual leader, Milton Friedman, had won the Nobel Prize in 1976—the essential structural characteristic required for successful application of monetarist precepts was becoming less and less valid. The "demand for money"—that is, people's desire to hold financial assets that could be used to buy goods, services, and other assets—ceased to behave in a stable fashion. This implied that stable money growth at moderate rates was no longer necessarily the route to steady, noninflationary real growth, since without a predictable demand for money, the Fed couldn't be sure that the rate of turnover of money in the economy, called the velocity of money, would behave in a predictable fashion.

In the mid-1970s, disturbances in the demand for money had started becoming large enough to complicate the Fed's job and to generate an active line of academic research.[4] By 1981 and 1982, deregulation and financial innovation—in the form of Negotiated

---

[4]The best-known article in this line is Stephen Goldfeld, "The Case of the Missing Money," *Brookings Papers on Economic Activity*, 1976:3, pp. 683–730.

Order of Withdrawal (NOW) accounts, money market mutual funds, and the like—had rendered the demand for money unstable.

This instability was exacerbated by the back-to-back nature of the 1980s recessions, which led households worried about their future employment prospects to attempt to "get liquid," trying to hold more money than the Fed had expected when it set its money growth targets for late 1981 and early 1982. As households sought to liquidate nonmoney assets to increase their money holdings, yields on nonmoney assets were driven up, slowing spending and making the recession worse. The Fed, itself confused as to how to interpret the money growth numbers, added to the economic slump by boosting interest rates as a matter of policy in February of 1982.

The Pragmatist Emerges

As discussed in Chapter 1, the deteriorating national and international economic situation led Volcker to refocus on the original and higher role of a central banker—to serve as a lender of last resort, as well as a regulator of the nation's money supply—and to change his monetarist tack. Interest rates plummeted by 400 basis points in the space of a few weeks, a bridge financing package leading to a more permanent restructuring was put in place for Mexico, and the bull market of the 1980s was on.

Of course, the fall in interest rates was accompanied by a substantial increase in money growth rates. Citing the expiration of All Savers Certificates, one-year obligations that were legislated as part of ERTA, Volcker stated that, in the remaining months of 1982, the monetary aggregates would be distorted. Funds flowing out of the certificates into checking accounts would balloon the aggregates well above their target ranges.

Thus, the pragmatic Fed chairman was able to have his cake and eat it too. He continued to give lip service to the monetarist principles that had been so useful in lowering expectations of inflation, while moving aggressively to lower interest rates to stave off international debt default and perhaps a global depression. To be sure, savvy market watchers knew, or thought they knew, exactly what Volcker was doing. But they couldn't be certain because in his spare public pronouncements he maintained that this departure from the monetary targets was a one-time phenomenon. Even if analysts were sure Volcker had turned away from monetarism, they took some comfort in the fact that so much excess capacity was available worldwide that there was little risk that inflation, now running at less than 4 percent, would pick up anytime soon.[5]

A Reputation Assessed

Paul Volcker thus entered the last year of his first term of office with the reputation of inflation-slayer *and* recession-ender. Certainly, the latter was true—as was the fact that Volcker's conversion to monetarism contributed strongly to the 1980 and 1981-to-1982 recessions.

As for the disinflation process, careful analysis of the historical relation between inflation and its sources—unemployment, expectations of inflation, and external causes (prices of oil and primary products, the dollar, and so forth)—suggests that the reduction of inflation experienced from 1979 to 1982 was about what one would expect from rising unemployment, a stronger dollar, and a stabilization of oil and commodity prices. Thus, apart from the credit earned as an inflation-tamer by creating higher unemployment, on the statistical evidence the Fed chairman deserves no "extra credit" for the credibility he brought to the inflation-fighting process.[6]

VOLCKER'S SECOND TERM: NEW CHALLENGES

As 1983 progressed, more and more attention was given to whether Paul Volcker would be reappointed by President Reagan. White

---

[5]Those of a monetarist persuasion, including Milton Friedman, were convinced that Chairman Volcker had been blowing smoke from his ubiquitous cigar all along. They cited the increased volatility of the money stock during Volcker's tenure as evidence that he had strayed from monetarist principles. Some of this volatility, of course, reflected shifts in the demand for money due to the shock of credit controls in 1980, as well as the popularity of a number of financial innovations and the development of new payments technology. James L. Pierce minimizes these effects and suggests that the Fed's unfamiliarity with reserves targeting in a setting of "lagged reserve accounting" led to an unstable supply of money. See *American Economic Review* 74 (May 1984), pp. 392–396, for a fuller discussion.

[6]For a more extensive discussion of the 1980s disinflation, see David McClain, "What Caused Inflation to Collapse? Stabilizing Oil and Farm Prices Hold the Key," *Challenge* 28 (September/October 1985), pp. 23–26.

House operatives, focusing on the 1984 election, feared the chairman's legendary independence of mind; he was lecturing them continually in congressional testimony about the evils of the deficits triggered by the failure to cut spending in line with the tax cuts contained in ERTA. Indeed, in mid-1982, the Tax Equality and Fiscal Responsibility Act (TEFRA) had been passed; it undid about $100 billion of the $750 billion in tax reductions contained in ERTA.

At the same time, the international debt situation remained problematic. Brazil, Argentina, and a number of other non-oil-producing Latin American countries also were experiencing payment- and debt-servicing difficulties; even extremely productive Korea was the object of some concern because of the size and rapid growth of its foreign debt.

There was plenty of blame to go around for this state of affairs. Bankers had lent too much, and developing nations had borrowed in excess, not expecting that the Fed's response to the second oil crisis would be different (fighting inflation) than its reaction to the first (attacking unemployment). The global recession, which attended moves toward monetary restriction in the United States, Japan, and Europe, had shrunk the growth of markets for the debtor nations' exports. The United States had responded to the 1981–1982 recession with a shift to easier money, and the "supply-side" tax cuts of ERTA were in fact—and fortuitously—being spent (just like all their predecessors). But abroad, fiscal restraint was the order of the day, so that markets outside of the United States were still growing slowly.

Further, even with the monetary relaxation of late 1982, the general fiscal stimulus and investment incentives contained in ERTA kept real interest rates in the United States high by historical standards. This boosted the dollar's value and—at a time when commodity prices had been falling for several years—made it quite difficult for developing nations to service their floating-interest-rate, dollar-denominated external debt.

In the end, the president feared that he couldn't afford to risk the political fallout and higher interest rates that might have accompanied the departure of a public official of Volcker's stature. Further, the fermenting international debt crisis and the risks it posed for the U.S. banking system meant that appointing the Fed Chairman again made economic as well as political sense. Finally, the requirements of the crisis made it unlikely that Volcker would move to tighten credit in the months before the 1984 election.

President Reagan announced the reappointment of Paul Volcker to a second term as Federal Reserve chairman on June 18, 1983.

Dodging the Debt Bullet

For most of the first two years of his second term, Volcker juggled keeping the domestic economy moving ahead, controlling the international debt crisis, and coping with the innovations being spawned (and the mergers and corporate restructurings under way) in the newly deregulated financial environment.

LDC debt problems after Mexico's near default were first tackled in the fashion that had become traditional in the postwar period. The International Monetary Fund's several "facilities" for financing payment imbalances were brought to bear on each country's problem. In return for the country's agreement to implement the necessary policies (usually, demand restraint) to get its payments situation under control, the Fund would disburse a loan intended to bridge the payments gap until the policy changes agreed upon began to bear fruit. With the IMF's stamp of approval on the country's economic policy program, commercial banks would come in and roll over existing loans and extend new credits. Each country's situation was handled on a case-by-case basis.

Clearly, this approach, originally envisaged as a route to take with a single country, would not work in the current environment of slow growth in the industrial nations, when not one but many developing nations were simultaneously in payment arrears. With many countries restricting domestic demand on the IMF's orders, multiplier effects muted growth in world production and trade, casting payment imbalance problems in an even harsher light. Calls began to be heard for a new, more comprehensive solution to the LDC debt crisis; some observers went so far as to suggest a "Marshall Plan" for Latin America.

Volcker resisted these overarching solutions and emphasized the need to continue to evaluate each country's problems individually, on its own merits. He was skeptical of the ability of a new institutional superstructure to operate with the flexibility required for such a crisis, and he realized the case-by-case approach gave more bargaining power to the banks. By 1985, however, reschedulings had become so tortuous and so frequent that both lenders and borrowers were intensifying their pursuit of a new way out. In this climate was born (with Volcker as midwife) what became, after Volcker's nemesis Donald Regan switched seats with James Baker, the Baker Plan discussed in Chapter 1. Essentially, the Baker initiative sought to have official capital committed for longer periods, through the World Bank and not the IMF, in return for growth-oriented "supply-side" policy changes rather than demand austerity.

A Bigger Casino

The mounting international debt problem had a spillover effect on the financial environment because it spawned the growth of one form of what has come to be called *securitization*.[7] In this process, corporations needing funds approach the market directly instead of taking out loans from now-more-risky (and more expensive) commercial banks that, because of the deteriorating quality of their loans (internationally as well as in such sectors as energy, shipping, real estate, and agriculture) have to charge more to attract deposits. Table 3–1 shows that securitized financing began to outstrip bank lending in international markets in 1983 and that the trend accelerated from 1984 to 1986.

Deregulation of financial markets also increased the competitive pressures on banks during the 1980s. The Depository Institutions Deregulation and Monetary Control Act of 1980 (DIDMCA) was largely a consequence of the high inflation experienced in the United States in the 1970s, but along with the phasing out of interest-rate ceilings came, in part through the 1982 Garn–St. Germain legislation, the beginnings of the relaxation of line-of-business and geographical restrictions on bank branching.

In Japan, the need to place larger and larger amounts of government debt at below-market yields with the government bond syndicate led the Ministry of Finance and the Bank of Japan to submit to pressure from banks and securities firms to open up Japanese cap-

---

[7]Portions of this section are based on "Global Financial Change," *World Financial Markets* (December 1986), p. 1–13, published by the Morgan Guaranty Trust Company.

TABLE 3–1
Gross International Borrowing (billions of dollars, annual rates)*

	1983	1984	1985	1986**
Securitized Financing	87	151	215	258
Bond Issues	77	122	168	232
Note Issuance Facilities	10	29	47	26
Syndicated Bank Loans	67	57	42	40
Other Backups	3	11	11	7
Total Borrowing	157	219	268	305
Memo: Securitized Fraction	55%	65%	80%	84%

*Data exclude merger-related standbys and renegotiations.
**1986 data for first 9 months.

Source: *World Financial Markets,* December, 1986. Used with permission of the copyright holder, Morgan Guaranty Trust Company of New York.

ital markets. Europe responded to the increasingly competitive domestic capital markets in North America and Japan by easing regulations as well. With deregulation came a wave of foreign investments in banking and finance, as indicated in Table 3–2.

Financial services firms responded to these competitive pressures by creating new products such as fee-based services (e.g., note-issuance facilities to address the rollover risk borrowers face

TABLE 3–2
The Growth of Foreign Banking by Host Country (number of foreign subsidiaries)

Country	1970	1980	1985
United States	50	579	783
United Kingdom	95	214	336
Germany	77	213	287
France	58	122	147
Switzerland	97	99	119
Japan	38	85	112
Luxembourg	23	96	106

Source: *World Financial Markets,* December 1986. Used with permission of the copyright holder, Morgan Guaranty Trust Company of New York.

in securitized markets) and by promoting off-balance-sheet activities such as interest-rate and currency swaps designed to permit borrowers and lenders to lay off the risk of more volatile inflation, interest, and exchange rates. Interest rate swaps totaled about $100 billion in mid-1985, $200 billion by early 1986, and on some estimates amounted to nearly $500 billion at the time of the Crash.

Scores of new products permitting the transference of risk were developed and traded on various exchanges in Chicago, New York, London, Singapore, and elsewhere using computer and communications technology not available a decade earlier. Figure 3–2 charts the explosive growth during this period in interest rate futures contracts, the most popular of the new instruments.

Not all of these innovations were successful; a new CPI futures contract, for example, never caught on. Steady inflation, a listing in Kansas City instead of Chicago, and the availability of interest rate futures probably were the reasons for its failure. Others, however, were "gushers" in the world of finance.

In addition to the T-bond and T-bill futures contracts, one would include in this category the contracts for future delivery of several leading indexes of stocks; of this group, the S&P 500 futures contract is perhaps the most famous. These index futures—indeed, the whole panoply of new, exchange-traded financial products— brought with them a new, derivative business opportunity: the exploitation of pricing anomalies between one new product and another, or between an old product and a new one. Stock index arbitrage, for example, arose to take advantage of disparities between the price of the S&P 500 futures contract and the cash prices of the stocks that make up the S&P 500.

The products' inventors, however, aware of regulatory and public concerns that these new instruments simply allowed wealthy individuals and institutions to gamble in more sophisticated ways, continued to emphasize their primary use, the hedging of risks. Indeed, as discussed in Chapter 5, the approval for trading of S&P 500 futures in 1982 provided a major boost to the acceptance by portfolio managers of a little-known hedging concept called "portfolio insurance," which promised to limit their exposure to stock market declines. Instead of liquidating their stock portfolios when the market headed down, portfolio insurance practitioners could sell the S&P 500 futures contract and achieve substantially the same objective with lower transactions costs

FIGURE 3–2
Interest Rate Futures' Explosive Growth

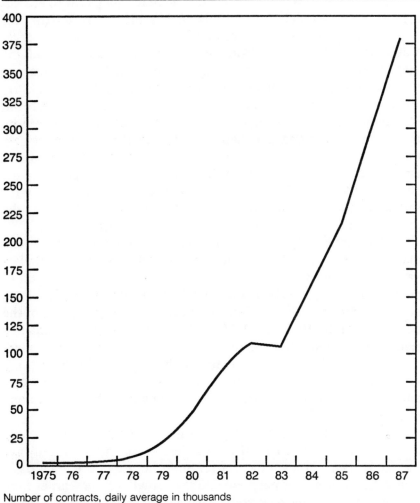

Number of contracts, daily average in thousands

Source: Annual reports of the Chicago Board of Trade and *World Financial Markets*, December, 1986, copyright the Morgan Guaranty Trust Company of New York.

Takeover Time and Domestic Debt Worries

While some stock market participants were learning how to protect against price declines, others—the risk arbitrageurs looking for undervalued companies—were betting on price advances. Merger waves are nothing new to American securities markets (recall the attractions of the conglomerate movement in the "go-go" years of the late 1960s). What distinguished the merger mania of the early 1980s, however, was not only its magnitude and extent—the result of significant structural adjustments in the economy triggered by the strong dollar and disinflation—but also the creation of new financial instruments (in particular, "junk" bonds) used to finance and effect the takeovers, as well as new strategies (poison pills, shark repellents, and the like) employed to defend a company (or rather, its management) from the raiders. Figure 3–3 describes the explosive increase in merger transactions in the early 1980s.

The increasingly fast and loose character of America's financial markets was mirrored in the statistics on debt accumulation. Harvard's Benjamin Friedman has found that since 1980 the ratio of debt to GNP in the U.S. economy has risen to nearly 1.7, a level not seen since the Depression.[8] Indeed, with the exception of the periods 1931 to 1935 and 1980 to 1987, this ratio has remained remarkably constant, at slightly less than 1.4, since the late nineteenth century. About 40 percent of the increase in the ratio is attributable to federal government borrowing, 10 percent to states and municipalities, and the remainder equally to households and business.

Household assets have risen to match the rise in household liabilities. Those who owe the liabilities, however, are not always the same ones who own the assets. Still, the use of credit cards as replacement means of payment and the growth of two-earner families mean that concerns about rising household debt-to-income ratios may be overstated.

Corporations, on the other hand, added to debt while equity—and assets—were on the decline as a percentage of GNP. In large

---

[8]See Benjamin Friedman, "Increasing Indebtedness and Financial Stability in the United States," National Bureau of Economic Research Working Paper, Number 2072, November, 1986.

FIGURE 3–3
Merger and Acquisition Activity in the United States, 1963 to 1987

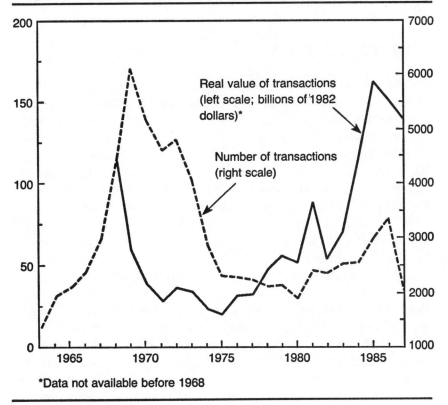

Real value of transactions (left scale; billions of 1982 dollars)*

Number of transactions (right scale)

*Data not available before 1968

Source: W. T. Grimm and Company.

part, Friedman traces these trends to the mergers, acquisitions, leveraged buyouts, and share repurchases of the last several years. Robert Taggart has observed that when market values rather than book values are used, corporations do not appear unduly leveraged in the mid-1980s. At 26 percent in 1983 and 27 percent in 1984, the debt-to-asset ratio for corporations was lower than in any year since 1972 and much lower than its peak of 38 percent in 1974.[9] On the other hand, in an economic environment characterized by structural adjustment, deregulation of several industries, and disinfla-

[9]See Robert Taggart, "Corporate Financing: Too Much Debt?" *Financial Analysts Journal* 42 (May/June 1986), pp. 35–42.

tion, one can't depend too much on old norms in assessing when corporate leverage is excessive.

HOW MUCH SAND IN THE MACHINERY?

Volcker responded cautiously but, as always, pragmatically to the increasingly casino-like atmosphere of American financial markets. Echoing his stratagem of August 1982, he used distortions in the checkable deposit component of Ml (caused by the commencement of interest payments on checking accounts and the consequent increase in the demand for money) to justify accelerating M1 growth into the double-digit range in 1985 and 1986, thereby prolonging the expansion that seemed to run out of steam midway through 1984 after the Fed's mild tightening. As noted in Chapter 2, in the spring of 1987, Chairman Volcker suspended the targeting of M1 for the same reason.

At the same time, Volcker moved against what he perceived as abuses of the rules of the takeover game. Under his leadership, the Federal Reserve took action in December 1985 to limit avoidance of Regulation G (governing margin credit), which occured via the use of "shell" corporations in takeover attempts. The Fed's ruling, which could be appealed on a case-by-case basis, was that all debt of such shell entities is presumed to be secured only by the stock of the target corporation and is thus subject to margin requirements.

On several occasions, the central bank used its regulatory authority to slow down the creation of "nonbank" banks (financial services institutions that are designated as banks because they either accept demand deposits or make commercial loans, but do not do both). And Volcker steadfastly opposed the repeal of the Glass-Steagall Act, which separates commercial and investment banking.

Was Paul Volcker the last stubborn little boy with his finger in the dike against the tide of financial innovation and deregulation? His argument was that the fragmented character of American financial services regulation required a congressional solution and that, as part of that solution, Congress should delineate the businesses, geographic territories, and different types of services various firms in the financial services industry are permitted to operate.

The polarization in attitudes in Congress on banking reform questions, however, between key committee chairmen Senator Jake Garn of Utah and Representative Fernand St. Germain of Rhode Island, paralyzed Congress throughout Volcker's second term. Some banking industry officials would say that's just what the wily Federal Reserve chairman wanted, thereby postponing to a more tranquil time the transition to a fully deregulated financial services industry.

Coping with the Dollar Cycle

Volcker's caution on financial deregulation was mirrored in his attitude toward the dollar, which came to be the central issue of his second term in the same way that inflation was the focus of his first. The growing technological and regulatory integration and internationalization of U.S. and foreign capital markets in the 1980s meant that, increasingly, monetary policy *was* exchange rate policy. This was particularly so after August 1982, from which point in time the Fed had *de facto* been using short-term interest rates as an operating target en route to some desired outcome, such as nominal GNP. U.S. yields relative to those in other national capital markets, in turn, strongly influenced current and future expected values of exchange rates because these markets were becoming increasingly integrated.

As he had with financial deregulation, Volcker sought to place on Congress (and the president) the responsibility for altering the path of economic policy to bring the dollar down and thereby to head off protectionist pressures. Through mid-1982, the dollar had risen by nearly 30 percent against the mark and 10 percent against the yen from its 1980 average levels; most of this appreciation could be attributed to the high interest rates and falling inflation rates (compared to those in other countries) that accompanied the Fed's monetarist experiment. As the economic recovery got under way, however, the dollar continued to rise; by mid-1984, it was up another 10 percent against the mark. This continued appreciation was largely the effect of the ever larger fiscal stimulus in ERTA, coming on stream in phases in October 1981, July 1982, and July 1983.

From that point through the end of 1984, aided initially by slightly tighter money and by a relaxation of withholding tax rules on foreign investors, the dollar continued to rise, by another 10 percent to 15 percent against most currencies. As the dollar's value became increasingly divorced from the fundamentals, however, the U.S. currency experienced a speculative bubble that grew and grew and then popped in February 1985.

Over the next eight months, the dollar gave up a good portion of the ground it had gained in the runup from mid-1984. After that, with the Plaza Agreement, the Louvre Accord, and the Tokyo economic summit in between, the Federal Reserve and the administration underscored their concern that the dollar's decline continue, that it be orderly, and that economic policies in the United States and abroad change expeditiously to allow these objectives to be achieved. As we have seen in Chapter 2, however, a smooth deflation of the dollar balloon proved increasingly difficult to achieve as 1987 wore on.

LEADERSHIP: THE SCARCEST COMMODITY

Students of history shivered when the announcement was made that Volcker would not continue as Fed chairman. They were acutely aware of the departure, in October 1928, of a similarly powerful personality from the Federal Reserve, and of the impact the leadership vacuum created by the death of Benjamin Strong had on the conduct of monetary policy during the months before the 1929 crash and the years after it.[10]

Strong had not been Fed chairman, but he was head of the Federal Reserve Bank of New York at a time when power in the Federal Reserve System was much more decentralized. Almost alone among Federal Reserve officials, he understood the lender-of-last-resort function of a central bank and appreciated the value of open-market operations in Treasury securities at a time when many of his contemporaries thought purchases of T-bills unsound, since no underlying commercial transaction was involved (this was called the "real bills" doctrine). With Strong's death, there was no single individual who combined the intelligence to understand

---

[10]On Strong's role, see Charles P. Kindleberger, *The World in Depression: 1929–39* (Berkeley: University of California Press, 1973), p. 296, and John Kenneth Galbraith, *The Great Crash* (Boston: Houghton Mifflin, 1961), pp. 333–34.

the appropriate exercise of Federal Reserve power with the assertiveness to take charge in a crisis.

Two Internationalists

Indeed, Strong's career in the 1920s and Volcker's in the 1980s demonstrate some striking parallels. Both men had been influential in engineering recessions at the beginning of their respective decades to snuff out inflation. As each decade progressed, Strong and Volcker both had taken an international perspective in the conduct of monetary policy. In the 1920s, Strong led Federal Reserve System efforts to facilitate the return of the British pound sterling to the gold standard by allowing the U.S. money supply to grow relatively rapidly. With American output per worker rising by 63 percent during the decade, an annual rate of 5 percent, this course risked little inflation.

Volcker in the 1980s was in a slightly different position, as the central banker of a country in relative decline (in the eight years of his tenure, output per worker hour grew by only 1.5 percent per year, far less than in Japan). His situation was most analogous to that of Montagu Norman, the Governor of the Bank of England in the late 1920s, and thus he was forced to be, as Norman had been, cautious about money supply growth. Still, after the buildup in the administration's deficits ceased in 1985, Volcker sought to supply sufficient liquidity to achieve an orderly reduction in interest rates and the dollar's value, with the ultimate objective of defusing the international debt crisis, reducing America's trade imbalance, and heading off protectionism.

At the end of both men's tenures at the Fed, the provisions of additional liquidity they had engineered in mid-decade had had only limited success in curing the problems to which they were addressed. Rather, reflecting the deflationary setting in each time, the initial impact of the extra liquidity seemed to be that it fueled financial, not real, investment.

Who's Minding the Store?

After Strong's death, the Federal Reserve's influence suffered at the hands of Charles Mitchell, the president of the National City

Bank and a new director of the Federal Reserve Bank of New York. In March 1929, impatient with the temporary gloom cast over the stock market by the Board of Governors' discussions about tightening credit, Mitchell went public with the statement: "If the Board won't make enough credit available to allow this prosperous nation to flourish, then my bank will." Such an end run on the board's authority would be unthinkable today, as would be the conflict of interest it raises. In fact, it would have been out of the question had Strong been alive and in the place of his successor, George Harrison. As discussed in Chapter 7, a similar lack of intelligent leadership afflicted the Fed, and as a result the economy, in 1930 and 1931, when the international monetary system was in crisis and the U.S. central bank had to walk the fine line between supporting the domestic economy and bolstering the external value of the dollar, and erred much too far in the latter direction.

To be sure, no one expected a George Harrison–style performance from Alan Greenspan. But knowledgeable observers were acutely aware of how useful Volcker's experience, prestige, and credibility as an inflation fighter had been at a time of such severe disruptions and imbalances in the world economy. Despite Greenspan's impeccable qualifications, he was not Paul Volcker, and the financial markets were nervous about the prospect of his stewardship over the nation's money supply and financial system.[11]

---

[11]For a less charitable view of Strong, and of Volcker, see William Greider, "Annals of Finance (the Fed)—Part III," The *New Yorker* (November 23, 1987).

CHAPTER 4

INTO THE VALLEY

Alan Greenspan, like George Bush in the 1988 presidential campaign, had the right resume for the job. His qualifications to replace Paul Volcker as Federal Reserve chairman, particularly in a Republican, private-sector-oriented administration, seemed nearly ideal. Christopher Caton, senior economist for Data Resources, a private forecasting firm, put it this way in *Fortune*: "He's ten inches shorter, but in other respects he's about as close to a Volcker clone as you can get." A self-made success in the highly competitive business-forecasting field, chairman of the Council of Economic Advisers under President Ford, head of the bipartisan commission that put Social Security on a sounder footing in the first Reagan administration—Greenspan had done it all.

He had even served as "scoutmaster" to the overly optimistic cadre of greenhorn, supply-side cubs whose first economic forecast in 1981 threatened to be so ludicrous as to destroy completely the credibility of the just-begun Reagan Revolution. Though still denigrated as the work of "Rosy Scenario," the forecast had been substantially toned down and spruced up (i.e., made internally consistent, if not externally plausible) under Greenspan's tutelage. The president had rewarded him not only with the Social Security assignment but also with the privileged status of being on call as an economic counselor.

Greenspan had two obvious liabilities coming into the job. He was a crackerjack domestic nonfinancial economist, intimately familiar with the data stream on the present and future prospects of the industrial sector in America; but this was a financial job, with both national and international dimensions, and he would have some work to do to come up to speed. Of greater concern was his close relationship with the administration. Investors feared that Greenspan would not be the aggressive inflation fighter that Volcker had been and that he might look the other way rather than squelch inflationary pressures if that meant slowing the economy before the November 1988 presidential election.

THE MARKET BOILS OVER

This concern was heightened in the 60 days between the announcement of Greenspan's appointment and August 8 when he actually took over, as the pace of economic activity quickened sharply. Orders were up strongly, the unemployment rate at 6 percent was at its lowest level since December 1979, and the monthly survey of the National Association of Purchasing Managers hit a 38-month high.

Stock prices also became increasingly inflated during this time, advancing from the 2300 level at the beginning of June to just below the 2600 mark in the first week of August. Stable-to-declining interest rates and a stronger dollar got the rally going; when bubbles of bad news appeared on trade, oil prices, Iran-Contra, and the Persian Gulf, the market shrugged them off. London and Tokyo also set more records during this period (indeed, in retrospect, London peaked), but as in the United States, volatility in these markets continued to be high, suggesting a global nervousness among investors. In the United Kingdom and the United States, interest rates resumed an upward trend as summer wore on, adding to the concern over markets some veterans described as "boiling."

Alan Greenspan's first fortnight on the job saw the Dow jump through the 2700 barrier, capping a rise of 300 points in 10 weeks. At the same time, inflation concerns were pushing the 30-year Treasury bond yields above 9 percent, a rise of 150 basis points in six months, and short interest was edging up against record levels.

The market's bubble finally burst on August 25, shortly after the release of surprisingly bad trade figures for June. Investors had been expecting no change or a slight improvement from the May level, which itself had been a disappointing $1 billion more in the red than April. Instead, reflecting a surging economy and continued stockpiling of oil inventories, the market got a further $1.7 billion

FIGURE 4–1
America's Deteriorating Merchandise Trade Performance

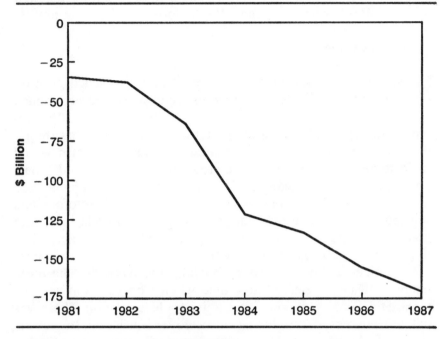

Source: *Survey of Current Business*, various issues.

deterioration in the trade account, to a $15.7 billion monthly deficit. Investors quickly concluded that the dollar must drop further to right the trade shortfall, that a weaker dollar would mean more inflation, and that more inflation would mean higher interest rates (see Figure 4–1).

Sentiment against the dollar also was building as interest rates rose in Germany and in particular in Japan. The almost spontaneous quickening in the pace of the Japanese economy caught Bank of Japan officials by surprise and triggered fears that inflation would rise above its tranquil 1 percent rate. Long-term bond yields had climbed from 3 percent to 6 percent in six months' time, and there was talk of boosting short-term rates—which put further pressure on rates in the United States.

Higher bond yields, in turn, would hurt equities in two time-honored ways: by leading investors to rebalance their portfolios away from the relatively low-yielding stocks and toward the increasingly attractive fixed-income securities; and by raising the cost of borrowing for consumers and businesses, in turn lowering their spending levels and diminishing the outlook for corporate profits.

Greenspan Counters

In the days after August 25, inflationary fears worsened. The release of the leading indicators at month's end suggested a continued acceleration of the pace of economic activity, and the healthy employment report published on September 4 promised that the industrial production data to be released at midmonth also would indicate more robust growth (the production data are based in part on employment information). The employment release contained a disquieting signal about wage inflation, which heretofore had seemed to be immune from the effects of a lower dollar: Average hourly earnings in August alone had risen 0.8 percent, according to preliminary estimates, roughly triple the pace of earlier months.

Political factors also were spooking the markets. The trade figures had been released at a time when Congress was moving toward final consideration of restrictive trade legislation. There was talk in Congress of introducing antitakeover legislation. In the Persian Gulf, shipping prospects were becoming dicier than ever. Tanker insurance premiums had risen by 50 percent, and the United States seemed to have gotten itself into an open-ended commitment escorting Kuwaiti oil shipments without having decided that it was truly ready to "stay the course."

Finally, as already noted, economic growth in Japan, and even in Germany, had shown signs of picking up further, with the result that the upward pressure on foreign yields continued. This helped to propel the dollar downward again (it had lost 7 percent from mid-August levels) and expectations of inflation upward.

Faced with these pressures, the Fed had begun to raise the federal funds rate, or at least to allow market pressures to drive it slightly upward. After the exchanges closed on September 4, the Fed took the confirming step of hiking the discount rate by half a point, to 6 percent; this was the first increase in the central bank's base lending rate since April 1984 (though Volcker had tried twice, without success, to get an increase in the spring of 1987). Commercial banks immediately parroted this action, boosting the prime half a point to 8.75 percent.

In a sense, Greenspan had little choice but to confirm so publicly the earlier federal funds rate increase he had engineered. He was the new kid on the inflation-fighting block; *both* he and the recently "retired" Volcker attended a meeting of central bankers at the Bank for International Settlements in Basle, Switzerland, in early September. As such, he had to fight at the first confrontation, demonstrating his inflation-fighting mettle.

A Costly Lesson in Discretion

Although his actions were appropriate in substance, in style they left something to be desired. Whenever Volcker had raised the discount rate, the official press release had cited "market conditions"—a conveniently vague term that left investors uncertain about exactly what was on the chairman's mind and preserved room for maneuvering. The September 4 announcement, however, specifically cited the Fed's concern over rising inflationary pressures. Perhaps Greenspan thought that such explicit language was necessary to show the markets that he was serious about fighting inflation. Whatever his intent, the effect was to reinforce the already deeply held concerns of professional money managers about the seriousness of the inflation problem.[1]

Greenspan also won few style points for his media appearances during his first two months in office. Though he initially followed the circumspect approach taken by Volcker, whose every public utterance had been calculated in advance, Greenspan began to wax expansive in his dealings with the financial press and the electronic media. To lay to rest growing concerns about inflation, he would enumerate all the ways in which inflation could get worse—rising commodity prices, a falling dollar, rising wages, increasing profit margins—and then assure the listener that *he* wasn't worried about a higher rate of price increase.

---

[1]David Wyss, chief financial economist of Data Resources, Inc., is the source of this insight.

Such an open and accessible style no doubt worked well for Greenspan when he was running his private-sector consulting firm. Perhaps it even fit in his earlier capacity as Chair of the President's Council of Economic Advisers; in the weeks and months after Watergate, candor and openness in government were at a particular premium.

But in the wake of Paul Volcker's departure, Greenspan simply couldn't get away with such an explicit listing of all the inflation risks, followed by his own personal assurance that all would be well. Perhaps Volcker could have carried such an open style off, given the credibility built up over eight years in office. With less than eight *weeks* under his belt, Greenspan would have been better advised to let aggressive antiinflation actions speak for themselves—and to keep to the "market conditions" line in official statements.

Every executive undergoes some on-the-job training. But it's particularly unfortunate that the chairmanship of the Federal Reserve had to change hands while the stock market was in such a speculative state. Rather than let the market down easily in the wake of rising concerns about inflation, no easy trick at any time, Greenspan's high-profile response boomeranged, making professional investors that much more worried about rising inflation, a weaker dollar, and higher interest rates.

LENGTHENING SHADOWS

The stock market slid sharply during the first trading session after the discount rate announcement, dipping 62 points to the 2500 level in intraday trading on Tuesday, September 8. With the July trade deficit figures, due out the next Friday, looming over the market, there was ample room for concern. But the market took the record $16.5 billion trade shortfall in its stride and roared back to close the week at 2609.

Preparations for the annual meetings of the IMF and World Bank at month's end refocused market watchers' attention on the level of cooperation among economic policymakers in the United States, Germany, and Japan. They knew that total central bank intervention to support the dollar under the Louvre Accord had been, at nearly $100 billion, roughly equal to the U.S. current-account deficit during that time. In other words, national economic policies were *still* so different that monetary authorities had been forced to provide *all* the financing of the American trade problem. In turn, this printing of marks and yen to buy dollars had ballooned German and Japanese money supplies, further exciting concerns over inflation in those countries.

Changes in national economic policies continued to be unconvincing. Congress passed a revised Gramm-Rudman law, which a reluctant president signed on September 30. But the markets quickly smelled the rat in this exercise, which postponed the timetable for deficit reduction by two years and put off all the hard choices until after the November 1988 presidential election. As one market observer put it, "Designing a fiscal straitjacket accomplishes little if its authors refuse to wear it."[2]

The Japanese too had come forth with yet another fiscal stimulus initiative. This time, six trillion yen (over $40 billion) was to be spent on increased public works and to be transferred to households and firms in the form of lower taxes. As with its predecessors, this program struck most observers as largely atmospheric and a repetition of the Japanese tendency to concentrate on form rather than substance. The Germans would have no part of any such politeness and stoutly refused to consider doing any more in the fiscal realm beyond the long-scheduled tax cuts set to be implemented at the beginning of 1988.

A Riskier Environment

In such a climate, the reaffirmation of the Louvre Accord at the annual meetings of the Fund and the Bank sounded hollow indeed. Rising interest rates in all the major industrial countries; an American president embattled over the controversial Supreme Court nomination of Robert Bork and embroiled in an increasingly dangerous and open-ended confrontation in the Persian Gulf; and the prospect of a change in Japanese leadership away from the internationally oriented Prime Minister Nakasone—all of these devel-

---

[2]Quoted in the *United and Babson Investment Report* (September 21, 1987), p. 374.

opments led investors to believe that the economic environment was becoming riskier and riskier.

The Americans were engaged in a game of "chicken" with the Japanese and the Germans to see who—the deficit-plagued United States or the surplus-blessed Germany and Japan—would blink first in moving to rebalance the international economy. At some point, the Americans might find it useful to threaten their trading partners by letting the dollar fall and the mark and the yen rise, thereby putting pressure on the politically important export lobbies in both countries. Alan Greenspan himself, before he had been nominated, had said that the dollar needed to decline at least another 10 percent to correct the U.S. trade deficit.

For much of 1987, investors had consoled themselves with the thought that if the Louvre Accord broke apart, a weaker dollar would give a permanent added fillip to corporate profits and only a temporary push to a higher rate of price increases. In the current environment of hypersensitivity to inflation, however, it was clear that another dollar decline could only mean an ever more vicious cycle of rising expectations of inflation, more upward pressure on bond yields, and less and less reason to hold stocks.

More Lights Turn Red

On Friday, October 2, 1987, the Dow-Jones industrials index stood at 2641, only 3 percent below its peak of five weeks earlier. In the week just ended, the seventh straight rise in the economy's index of leading economic indicators and another surprisingly strong employment report had stoked the inflation fires further, but the market seemed to have learned to live with bond yields in the 9.5 percent vicinity.

On Monday, October 5, however, Japanese long-term bonds rose another notch, to a high for the year of 6.2 percent, and the purchasing managers' report for September indicated strong growth (and more inflation) ahead. As pressure on the dollar mounted and inflation fears worsened, U.S. long yields increased to 9.8 percent. The next day, commercial banks raised their prime lending rate another half point, to 9.25 percent, making a full point rise in the prime in little more than 30 days.

On Tuesday, October 6, the Dow lost 91 points, a record in absolute terms. Perhaps investors had been influenced by guru Robert Prechter's change of heart, as he revised his outlook to call for a 300-point drop in the Dow before the rise to 3500 could resume. By week's end, long-term bond yields in Germany had risen to a peak of 6.9 percent, and the Bundesbank had increased its securities repurchase rate to 3.6 percent from 3.5 percent, citing inflation worries. The Bank of Japan urged banks there to disburse credit more cautiously. With tighter money abroad convincing U.S. analysts that stiffer credit conditions in the domestic market couldn't be avoided, the market's most famous barometer settled at 2482, 6 percent below its level seven days earlier.

Federal Reserve Chairman Greenspan had tried during this week to address concerns about inflation, but again his choice of words ended up making investors more, not less, concerned: "There is no real economic reason for resurgent inflation, but if enough people expect it, that expectation alone could boost money rates."[3]

Across the Pacific, America's misfortune seemed to be Japan's good luck, at least in the minds of investors. Expecting that a stronger yen would permit lower interest rates in the future, they propelled the Nikkei index past its previous peak of 26118 and on into new territory. In London, where rising yields had pulled the *Financial Times* index back from its 1987 top of 1926, a more measured correction continued.

THE PARTY'S OVER

The events of October's first week convinced Wall Street that the long bull market of the 1980s truly was at an end. With the dollar appearing to be falling off the Louvre Accord table, and interest rates under upward pressure in Germany and Japan, the Street's investment bankers knew that the days of easy inventory profits from trading securities in a market of lower interest rates were gone, if not forever, then for long enough for them to pare some

---

[3]Quoted in the *United and Babson Investment Report* (October 13, 1987), p. 403.

of their over-bloated staffs. Alan Greenspan's Fed was going to have to, as former Fed Chairman William McChesney Martin was fond of saying, "take away the punch bowl just when the party was getting good," whether it wanted to or not: Foreign investors demanded such teetotaling action if they were to continue to finance America's trade deficit.

Investment banks also noticed, with some alarm and a sense of resignation, the Federal Reserve chairman's first step out from under Paul Volcker's long shadow. In congressional testimony delivered October 5, Greenspan stated his approval of the notion that commercial banks should be allowed to underwrite securities as long as that side of their business was not protected by federal deposit insurance. Given a change of heart by long-time opponent of deregulation Senator William Proxmire and the support of Greenspan's position by the "retail" investment banks such as Merrill Lynch, the old-line wholesale investment bankers, whose lifestyles had made them the Gatsbys of the 1980s, knew that their era was on the wane.

America's commercial banks were only a little cheered by Greenspan's public support for the elimination of the Glass-Steagall Act. Their attention was focused on the continuing and intensifying problem of international debt. To raise cash to cover those aggressive LDC debt write-offs, Citibank had been forced to sell part of its New York headquarters to a Japanese insurance company. At the annual meetings of the IMF and the World Bank, word was heard that one or more of the big German banks might unilaterally forgive a significant fraction of its loans to Brazil; Deutsche Bank's reserves against LDC loans were reputed to be 70 percent of the total, more than twice the level of the typical American bank. This fragmentation of the creditors group would strengthen the hand of the large Latin American debtors, all of whom were queued for another round of rescheduling.

Despite these disturbing developments, the economic picture did have some positive features as October ended its first week: Canada and the United States had succeeded in negotiating the outline of a new bilateral free-trade agreement; an expected slowdown in U.S. auto sales was looked to as insurance that any inflationary pressures under way would not build; and Treasury Secretary James Baker and his British counterpart, Chancellor of the Exchequer Nigel Lawson, had just put forth a proposal—involving tying global money growth to commodity prices—designed to re-place the Louvre Accord with an ongoing system to regulate the conduct of monetary policy among nations, and thus more auto-matically eliminate trade imbalances.

The win-some, lose-some, business-as-usual mood was ex-emplified by reports of a survey of the members of the National Association of Business Economists, who were said to expect 3 percent real growth in 1987, and 2.7 percent in 1988, with no reces-sion threatening the economy before 1989. Like the inhabitants of Pearl Harbor on Thanksgiving Day, 1941, most investors were con-cerned, but not alarmed, about the situation. The near-term course of the economy and the stock market would be risky, but not catastrophic. Among those few who foresaw the carnage to come, many were, as Columbia University's Louis Lowenstein put it, "staying for one last drink."[4]

SLIDE TO THE ABYSS

Ironically, the path to the Crash of 1987 began with congressional attempts to act in a fiscally responsible fashion, trying to meet the revised Gramm-Rudman targets it had set for itself. On Monday, October 12, reports from Washington of a $12 billion tax package being put together by the Democrats on the House of Represen-tatives Ways and Means Committee mentioned that a little-known feature under consideration, worth millions, not billions, of dollars, would change the tax accounting rules governing mergers. The deductibility of interest used to finance acquisitions would be capped at $5 million; successful takeovers would be subject to an additional tax; and investors receiving "greenmail"—capital gains from a cor-porate raid fought off by current management—would have to pay a nondeductible excise tax on the proceeds. Though this measure had not been formally incorporated into the package, it led some investors to consider unwinding positions in the stocks of takeover target firms. Still, the Dow edged above 2500 in light trading on Tuesday.

---

[4]Quoted in the *New York Times* (December 13, 1987), p. 44.

The August trade figures, to be released on Wednesday, October 14, were awaited with much anticipation. The market consensus was that an improvement from July's record red ink was in the cards; most observers thought the trade deficit would come in around the $14 to $14.5 billion level. Instead, a shortfall of $15.68 billion was reported, a rebound of only $0.8 billion from July. Investors immediately concluded that the dollar would have to drop more than had been expected to rectify the trade problem and that in the face of this possibility foreign capital would have to be offered higher yields to stay on or to come to America's shores—*if* the Federal Reserve was serious about maintaining exchange rates in the range agreed upon at the Louvre. If the Fed wanted the dollar lower, lower it would go—and inflame expectations of inflation on the way down.

Shortly after the trade figures were released, news came that the antitakeover provisions had been formally included in the House tax legislation. This report, and the "damned-if-you-do, damned-if-you-don't" prospects for the dollar, pushed long-term bond rates above 10 percent on Wednesday for the first time since December 1985. Short yields rose nearly half a point, and stocks dropped 44 points in the first half hour, finishing the day down a record 95 points.

The next day, foreign stock markets experienced significant selling pressure, and Chemical Bank boosted its prime rate another half point, to 9.75 percent. Treasury Secretary Baker expressed concern about yet another increase, to 3.85 percent, in the securities repurchase rate by the Bundesbank, charging that it was not "reflective of the spirit of our recent consultations,"[5] and intimated that the United States might have to let the dollar fall below the implicit Louvre Accord bands.

In response, interest rates rose further in trading described as "wild," and the Dow, having come back from down 20 at the opening to be off only 4 points at 3:30, went into a free-fall in the last half hour, finishing the day off 57 points. Trading volume on Thursday soared to 263 million shares as market observers detected a sharp increase in portfolio insurance activity (portfolio insurance and stock index arbitrage will be discussed in detail in Chapter 5).

---

[5]Quoted in *The Wall Street Journal* (October 16, 1987), p. 21.

The Dow capped the week with a record 108-point, 4.6 percent plunge on Friday, October 16, on a historic high volume of 338 million shares. Down only 7 points at 11 A.M., the average fell 30 points in the next hour as another wave of portfolio insurance sales of stock index futures triggered index arbitrage programs that pushed down the value of stocks. A second episode of selling pressure snuffed out a brief rally, and the Dow lost another 70 points by 2 P.M. After another technical rebound, a third wave of liquidation pared 50 points more from the index's value between 3:30 and 3:50. But in the last 10 minutes of trading, the Dow came back 22 points·

At the Edge

The Dow's decline by over 250 points, or more than 10 percent, during the period October 14 to October 16 was the quickest substantial market correction most of those working on the Street had ever seen. The selling triggered by antitakeover legislation, the merchandise trade figures, and Treasury Secretary Baker's spat with the Germans reverberated through the market. Investors also were shaken by the first direct hit on an American-registered tanker in Kuwaiti waters. Though the tanker was not under actual American escort, most analysts felt the attack presented the president with the dilemma of risky retaliation or embarrassing inaction. On the news, oil futures surged nearly 50 cents.

Portfolio insurers, whose formulae call for sales of futures equivalent in value to 20 percent of the portfolio being hedged for every 10 percent decline in market values, were a growing factor. On Wednesday and Thursday, they were in the market episodically, on a few occasions accounting for 15 percent of S&P 500 futures volume; at Thursday's opening, they made up 25 percent. On Friday, however, their presence was more continuous and persistent (see Figure 4–2), at times amounting to over 35 percent of all contracts traded.

Despite this sharp step-up in activity, at Friday's final bell those close to the market could tell that the firms providing portfolio insurance, who were said to cover $60 to $90 billion in equity assets, had not been able to execute all the sales of futures dictated by their formulae. One rough estimate made later by Crash investigators put the amount to be sold at $12 billion (at a minimum), 20 percent of at least $60 billion under management, based on a 10

FIGURE 4–2
S&P 500 Index and Futures Contract, and Portfolio Insurance Activity on Friday, October 16, 1987

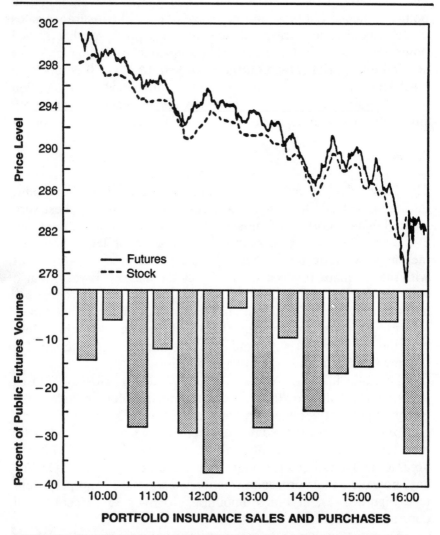

percent correction in the market. Through the close of business Friday, only $4 billion had been sold.[6]

Even that amount of trading late Friday had made many market veterans nervous, because it appeared that the volume of stock and stock index futures trading had been so large as to temporarily overwhelm the market-making systems on the New York Stock Exchange and the Chicago Mercantile Exchange (CME). The symptom of this problem was the unusually wide spread that opened between the Standard & Poor's index of 500 stock prices and the futures contract on that index traded on the CME. Relatively quickly, however, the gap closed, and the S&P 500, like its smaller and less representative Dow counterpart, finished the day off about 5 percent.

Still, $8 billion in stock index futures remained to be sold. These ordered-but-not-yet-made sales provided a wonderful opportunity for market insiders. If these so-called "frontrunners" could sell *their* stocks *before* portfolio insurers dumped futures (to index arbitrageurs, who, as discussed in Chapter 5, would buy the futures and sell the actual stocks), they could profit by buying the stocks back later at lower prices. Thus, as the weekend of October 17 and 18 began, Wall Street participants knew that a substantial amount of selling pressure was hanging over the market.

Loose Lips Sink Ships

It's not clear that the market mechanism could have absorbed all this pressure without falling apart under any circumstances. But Treasury Secretary Baker didn't help matters with his decision to go public, through remarks attributed to a staffer, in the Sunday issue of the *New York Times* with the statement that the United States had decided to allow the dollar to decline if market pressures (i.e., higher German interest rates) dictated. Baker followed those disembodied words with the assertion in real time on NBC's Sunday public affairs program "Meet the Press," "We will not sit back in this country and watch surplus countries jack up their interest rates and squeeze growth worldwide on the expectation that the United States somehow will follow by raising its interest rates."[7]

---

[6]Estimate from the *Report of the Presidential Task Force on Market Mechanisms* (Washington: U.S. Government Printing Office, 1988), p. 29.

[7]Quoted in the *New York Times* (October 19, 1987), p. D5.

If there's a lesson that American officials have not learned in the era of floating exchange rates, it's that the dollar will go down if you talk it down (the converse, regrettably, has proven decidedly untrue, though not for lack of trying). A corollary of this fact is that the dollar will go down faster if two American officials, or an American official and a foreign official, with whom the American has an allegedly binding agreement, express different sentiments about where they want the currency to be.

The markets thought they heard in Baker's comments what they had long suspected—the last gasps of the Louvre Accord, so stirringly endorsed at the end-of-September meeting of the IMF. The breakdown in international economic cooperation symbolized by Baker's remarks sent shock waves through the international financial community, for it called into question—as his public dispute with Paul Volcker had done at the beginning of 1987—the prospect for a reasonably stable dollar in the weeks and months ahead.

Over the weekend of October 17 and 18, sentiment elsewhere in the financial electronic and print media was at its most bearish since the 1982 recession. The *New York Times* intoned in its Sunday business section, "While the 17.5 percent decline thus far from the August high of 2722.42 might be viewed as just a monstrous correction in an ongoing bull market, many investors may be unable to think of it as anything but a reminder of an earlier October massacre—the Crash of 1929."[8]

The industrial nations, and professional money managers, had no stomach for a "son-of-Louvre" accord that did not back up noble sentiments with specific policy actions. German-U.S. differences over who should go first, and by how much, had broken into the open, as Texan Baker had mimicked the showdown with foreign governments and investors engineered by the last Treasury Secretary from Texas, John Connally, that broke up the Bretton Woods system of fixed exchange rates. The only difference, but a critical one, was that the United States was now dealing from a much

---

[8]From Andrew Feinberg, "Looking for a Silver Lining," *New York Times* (October 18, 1987), Business Section, p. 1.

weaker balance-of-payments position, and hence had a much greater reliance on foreign investors.[9]

It seemed unlikely that these disagreements could be resolved soon. The upshot was that investing in stocks and other financial assets had become much riskier because the future values of national currencies—the ever more essential languages of commerce in the increasingly global capital markets—had become much more uncertain. It was as though the rules for translating French into German, and English into Japanese, had been changed—but no one was quite sure what the new translation rules were.

---

[9]David Hale's *Weekly Money Report* (Chicago: Kemper Financial Services) of October 19, 1987, is the source of this comparison of Texan Treasury Secretaries.

CHAPTER 5

APOCALYPSE ON WALL STREET

The early fall had been a rough one for weather. An earthquake measuring 6.1 on the Richter scale rocked Los Angeles at the end of September, Japan had to cope with the usual minor tremors, and on October 16 a freak hurricane swept over Britain, killing a score of people. In an eerie analogy to and foretaste of Black Monday, the experts at the British meteorological office had failed to forecast the gusts of over 100 miles per hour until just before they arrived.

OCTOBER 19: PRELUDE

Not so inside the trading rooms of brokerage firms and on the floors of the stock and futures exchanges around the world, where the storm clouds looked more than ominous and some wags said computers were poised on window ledges. The Japanese market had only a mildly negative reaction to the bad news of the weekend, as the Nikkei 225-stock index lost 2.5 percent of its value on October 19 on low volume. Sydney, too, posted a substantial, but not catastrophic, 3.7 percent decline. In Singapore, however, the *Straits Times* index plummeted 12.1 percent, while traders in Hong Kong sheared 11.1 percent off the market index there.[1]

---

[1]Several accounts have been particularly useful in reconstructing the events of the day of the Crash and its aftermath. In particular, I have used "Behind the Great Crash of '87," *Boston Globe* (December 22, 1987), pp. 47, 56–58; the four-part series "The Crash of '87," *The Wall Street Journal* (December 11, 16, 29, and 30); "Terrible Tuesday: How the Stock Market Almost Disintegrated a Day after the Crash," *The Wall Street Journal* (November

In London, where the Friday hurricane had all but closed the market, unit trust managers found themselves coping with heavy selling pressure with only Thursday's closing prices to guide them, then watched in dismay as the Ordinary Index sank and then rose at the rate of 100 points per hour. Guru Robert Prechter was said, incorrectly as it turned out, to have warned of a plunge in the Dow to 1200 to 1300 if it fell below his estimated "support range" of 2040 to 2120; the range was reported accurately. Treasury Secretary Baker was reported, correctly, to have stopped in Frankfurt en route to a planned week-long visit to Belgium, Denmark, and Sweden to try to kiss and make up with his German counterpart, Gerhard Stoltenberg.

Amidst the uncertainty, the London market was off nearly 9 percent at the close. Blue chip stocks bore the brunt of the selling pressure, some of which was reported to have come from the United States as American mutual fund managers sought to beat the expected wave of selling in New York. On the Continent, the Paris Bourse lost 6.1 percent of its value, Frankfurt was off 7.8 percent, Milan 6.3 percent, and Amsterdam 7.8 percent.

Even before the 9:30 opening bell in New York, traders were hit with another dose of bad news (besides a mountain of foreign sell orders) as the wire services reported around 7 A.M. that two Iranian oil platforms had come under fire from U.S. forces. In Chicago, the Mercantile Exchange's S&P 500 December futures contract opened down 7 percent from Friday's close, while the Chicago Board of Trade's Major Market Index value at 9:15 presaged an immediate 3 percent, or 70-point, fall in the Dow.

Six hours and 45 minutes later, such an outcome would have been more than welcome. In a cataclysm that promises to echo across decades, eras, and perhaps even centuries, the Dow Jones Industrial Average lost 508 points, or 22.6 percent of its value, on record trading volume of 604 million shares (a full one-third greater than the maximum for which the NYSE had planned), worth $21 billion. The setback dwarfed the 12.8 percent one-day fall on Monday, October 28, 1929, and sent shock waves around the globe.

20, 1987); and the *Report of the Presidential Task Force on Market Mechanisms* (Washington: U.S. Government Printing Office, 1988). To a lesser extent, I have used the reports of the General Accounting Office (GAO), the Commodity Futures Trading Commission (CFTC), the New York Stock Exchange (NYSE), and the Securities and Exchange Commission (SEC).

Contemporaneously, the Canadian and Mexican exchanges also set records for one-day losses. In Toronto, the market index fell 9.1 percent, more than the 7.7 percent 1940 standard, while the Mexican market, the hottest of 1987, lost 16.5 percent of its value.

In the aftermath of the Crash of 1987, analysts would point to three proximate, and not necessarily mutually exclusive, explanations for the market's calamity.[2] Certainly the economic environment had become riskier over the weekend, and investors must be compensated for higher risks with higher returns on stocks: That means lower stock prices. On one calculation based on traditional models of market valuation, if stocks were perceived as 25 percent riskier on Monday than they were on Friday, then given current levels of interest rates, stock prices would have had to fall by 20 percent to generate the higher returns necessary to compensate investors for the higher risk.

A second explanation focused on the breakdown of the system for trading stocks on October 19 (and October 20) and the role that breakdown had in sending investors fleeing to the exits. A third line of inquiry, much loved by the media but also given prominence by the Presidential Task Force on Market Mechanisms, would center on the roles of computers and exotic new financial instruments and strategies, such as portfolio insurance and stock index arbitrage. The media accounts would paint in lavish detail a portrait of an investing public fallen prey to its own mindless creations.

Portfolio Insurance: Investors' Fountain of Youth

Portfolio insurance programs, as noted in the preceding chapter, had been in the news since the preceding Wednesday and certainly played a leading role in the abrupt decline in the stock market on October 19. The concept of portfolio "insurance," invented in 1976 by Hayne Leland, a professor of finance at the business school of the University of California at Berkeley, originally called for portfolio managers to hedge, or "insure," the value of their stocks by

---

[2]This schema is from Hayne Leland, "Portfolio Insurance and the October 1987 Market Decline," presented at the 1987 Annual Meeting of the American Economic Association, Chicago, December 29, 1987.

buying in a rising market and selling in a falling one, parking the cash from the portfolio sales in an interest bearing account and counting on the interest to limit the portfolio's losses.

With the advent of the S&P 500 futures contract in May 1982, the portfolio insurance concept, already being marketed by LOR Associates (Leland's firm, with partners John O'Brien and Berkeley professor Mark Rubinstein), became much easier to implement. If a portfolio sponsor observed a decline in the overall market and thus in the value of the stocks accumulated by its managers, it simply "locked in" the value of the market component of the return on its portfolio by selling a prescribed number of S&P 500 futures contracts.

(A futures contract is an agreement to receive or deliver a commodity or cash at an agreed-upon time in the future, at a price decided on today. The S&P 500 futures contract is priced based on the value of the 500 stocks that make up the S&P 500 index. The price is not exactly the same as the price of the underlying stocks in the index; differential margin requirements, the time value of money between now and the "delivery" of the contract, and the dividend status of the stocks all contribute to the pricing differential.)

In essence, portfolio insurance is just a very sophisticated way to limit one's losses in a declining market. As such, it is the big brother of the widely practiced "stop-loss" directive investors leave with their brokers, instructing them to close out a position (i.e., sell stock for cash) if the stock's price declines below the stop level. Both stop-loss provisions and portfolio insurance are voluntary trading rules. One involuntary rule is the margin call, which forces out of the market the individual who can't put up sufficient additional margin.

With the development of increasingly sophisticated computer systems, portfolio insurance's popularity grew exponentially after 1985, to the point that, as mentioned in Chapter 4, between $60 and $90 billion in assets were covered in mid-October 1987. As stock prices declined sharply in the days after October 14, more and more portfolio insurance "programs" were activated. Thus, on the morning of October 19, the queue to sell the S&P 500 futures contract on the CME was long, forcing the price of the futures contract down by 7 percent immediately.

Brownouts and Stock Index Arbitrage

As portfolio insurance had grown in popularity, professionals had become concerned about two potential problems its widespread use could cause. The first was the liquidity effect, analogous to the power brownouts caused on hot days in the summer when everyone turns on their air conditioners at the same time. If the utility hasn't built enough generating capacity (i.e., if the market makers, called "locals" in the futures markets, on the exchanges don't have enough access to capital), then power delivery stops and no one can use air conditioners (i.e., it becomes impossible to activate the portfolio insurance strategy by selling S&P 500 futures). Said another way, if everyone wants to become a seller, then the CME has to have enough capital to be the buyer—and that's a lot of capital.

The second risk professionals saw was a potentially unhealthy way portfolio insurance could interact with another new, computer-based trading technique, "stock index arbitrage." The brainchild of, among others, former MIT mathematics professor and blackjack wizard, Ed Thorp, stock index arbitrage was simple and essentially riskless. One just compared the value of all the stocks in the S&P 500 with the value of the futures index and adjusted for the reasons, mentioned above, that one should differ from the other. If this adjusted comparison showed that futures were cheaper, then the stock index arbitrageur would buy them and sell the underlying stocks. If futures were dearer, then they were sold and the stocks were bought. The idea was very much like buying a new car on sale and then selling it to someone else for full price.

In the case of stock index arbitrage, the effective implementation of this strategy required powerful computers to make the necessary calculations quickly and then to send the orders through the computerized trading system run by the NYSE and the AMEX, called the "designated order turnaround" or DOT system. As more and more institutional investors caught on to the possibilities of stock index arbitrage, the opportunities to profit from disparities in the price of the S&P 500 stocks themselves (the "cash" price) and the futures price diminished, and larger and larger trades were required to make the same amount of money. Increasing arbitrage volume flowed through the DOT system, and it was upgraded, enlarged, and rechristened SuperDOT.

The unhealthy interaction of portfolio insurance and stock index arbitrage would work as follows: Portfolio insurers, observing a drop in the stock market, would sell stock index futures, driving down their price. This would make futures cheap, relative to the S&P 500 basket of 500 stocks, causing stock index arbitrageurs to buy the futures and sell the stocks, driving down stock prices.

This decline in stock prices was just what had triggered the portfolio insurance strategies in the first place and would set in motion a second round of portfolio insurance–based sales of stock index futures. This would lead stock index arbitrageurs to buy the cheaper futures and sell the stocks, driving down stock prices still further and calling into play even more portfolio insurance programs.

In this interaction, it's important to realize that in the absence of S&P 500 index futures, the portfolio insurers would simply sell the stocks themselves; such activity is called "straight" program trading. Thus, the index arbitrageurs serve merely as the transmission mechanism to the stock market for the selling pressure that originates in the portfolio insurance management strategy.

ANATOMY OF A MELTDOWN

On the morning of October 19, this is exactly what was happening to the Dow and the broader market indexes. With the futures index at such a substantial apparent discount to the S&P 500 stocks themselves, stock index arbitrageurs were buying futures and dumping stocks with a vengeance. Foreign sales orders; straight sell programs sent through SuperDOT by a few portfolio insurers permitted by their clients to sell stocks as well as futures; and stock sales triggered by mutual fund redemptions at a small number of fully-invested firms all added to the extreme downward pressure on stocks, as did the morning rise in the yield on 30-year Treasuries to 10.45 percent. The selling pressure was so severe that by 10:30 A.M. only 19 of the 30 stocks in the Dow Jones had opened for trading (see Table 5–1). Based on those that had opened, the Dow had lost 100 points from Friday's close and stood at around the 2150 level.

The problem in part was with the "specialist" system employed by the NYSE. Each specialist is charged with making a

TABLE 5–1

Trading in the 30 Dow Industrials During the Oct. 19 Crash

Company	Friday Oct. 16 Close	Monday Oct. 19 Time of Opening	Monday Trading		
			Change at Opening	Day's Price Change	Intraday Trading Gaps*
Union Carbide	27⅜	9:31	− 1⅛	− 2⅜	None
USX Corp.	34	9:35	− 1¾	−12½	None
Bethlehem Steel	16½	9:36	− ¾	− 5⅛	None
AT&T	30	9:36	− 1⅝	− 6⅜	None
Boeing	43⅝	9:41	− 1¾	− 5⅛	None
International Paper	46⅜	9:44	− 5⅜	−12½	None
Chevron	49½	9:44	− 2	− 8¼	None
Woolworth	42¼	9:45	− 1¼	− 6	10 min.
United Technologies	48⅝	9:46	− 2⅛	− 7⅝	None
Allied-Signal	39⅛	9:48	− 3⅝	−11½	None
General Motors	66	9:49	− ⅝	− 6	None
Procter & Gamble	85	9:51	− 3	−23⅝	None
Coca-Cola	40½	9:54	− 4¼	−10	None
McDonald's	43⅝	9:56	− 3⅛	− 7¼	None
Minnesota Mining	70¼	9:55	− 6¼	−14¼	None
Primerica	44⅜	9:58	− 3	−10¼	8 min.
Navistar	6	10:15	− ⅛	− 1⅛	None
General Electric	50¾	10:30	− 8¾	− 8⅞	None
Westinghouse	60½	10:36	− 9½	−20¼	None
Alcoa	56	10:39	− 5	−13½	None
Kodak	90⅛	10:40	−14⅛	−27¼	10 min.
Texaco	36½	10:42	− 4½	− 4½	None
IBM	135	10:43	−13	−31¾	None
Merck	184	10:47	−22	−24	30 min.
Philip Morris	102¾	10:48	−12¾	−14⅝	None
Du Pont Co.	98½	10:56	− 8½	−18	None
Sears Roebuck	41½	10:58	− 4¾	−10½	None
Goodyear Tire	59½	10:58	− 6½	−17	None
Exxon	43¾	11:23	− 3¾	−10¼	6 min.

*Amount of time that stock did not trade during day

Source: *The Wall Street Journal* (December 16, 1987), p. 20.

market in a certain number of stocks, buying or selling from its own account to smooth out order imbalances. Few of these firms, however, were sufficiently capitalized to cope with the extreme volume of October 19. As an example, the firm making a market for USX, Shell, and 25 other firms had capital of $12 million and access to credit of another $40 million. Yet orders in USX and Shell alone totaled $250 million on that day.[3]

The inability of stocks to open hampered attempts by stock index arbitrageurs to gauge the relative positions of the S&P 500 stocks in the cash market and the December S&P 500 futures contract. Many entered sell-at-market orders through SuperDOT, reflecting the large apparent premium of stocks over futures. When, by 11 A.M., all but one of the stocks in the Dow had opened, more accurate comparisons were possible, and arbitrage activity returned the futures market to its more normal relationship with the cash market—to a premium. The Dow at this point was down over 200 points, but in the next hour it rallied by nearly 100 as investor sentiment firmed (see Figures 5–1 and 5–2).

By this time, volume in the stock market was running at 200 million shares—a normal day's work in less than a morning. Delays of an hour in the execution of orders through SuperDOT were occurring, as a few portfolio insurers continued to augment their selling of S&P 500 futures with straight sell programs. In particular, the notification of specialists of SuperDOT orders via high-speed printers was slowed by equipment limitations and software problems.

Arbitrage Short-Circuited

The breakdown in the SuperDOT system created enormous problems for stock index arbitrageurs seeking to buy relatively cheap futures and sell the underlying stocks. Such strategies require split-second execution to be riskless and profitable. With such long delays in selling stocks in a declining market environment, arbitrageurs couldn't be sure that when settlement was finally made, they wouldn't have sold stocks for less than the futures cost them.

Those arbitrageurs who kept minimal inventories of stocks, and most did, also were hampered in executing their strategy by the exchange's regulations, promulgated in the wake of the 1929 crash, concerning short selling in a declining market. In order to execute the buy futures/sell stocks strategy, the arbitrageurs had to sell borrowed stock (i.e., sell short). But to be able to do so,

---

[3]From the *New York Times* (December 20, 1987).

FIGURE 5–1

S&P 500 Index and Futures Contract, and Portfolio Insurance Activity on Monday, October 19, 1987

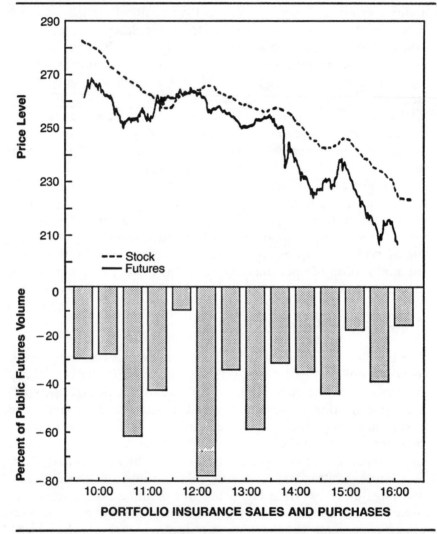

Source: *Report of the Presidential Task Force on Market Mechanisms* (Washington: Government Printing Office, 1988), p. 31.

FIGURE 5–2
**Dow Jones Industrials One-Minute Chart, Index Arbitrage, and Straight
Program Activity, on Monday, October 19, 1987**

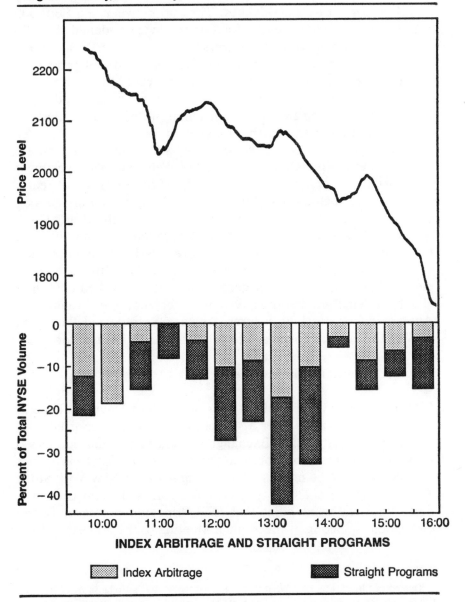

Source: *Report of the Presidential Task Force on Market Mechanisms* (Washington: Government
Printing Office), p. 32.

regulations required that they wait for an uptick in the stock's price, which of course never came.

Thus, by early afternoon, most stock index arbitrage activity had been forced to the sidelines. The gap between the S&P 500 and the December futures contract on the index widened steadily, as a small group of portfolio insurers trying to sell S&P 500 futures found no buyers. Some then resorted to straight sell programs. Other traders, unable to gauge the current level of the cash market because of trading delays, resorted to the futures market and based their offer prices on the steadily declining futures price, thereby sucking the cash prices further downward.

Despite the market's disruptions, some portfolio insurers pressed ahead. Fred Grauer, the head of Wells Fargo's Investment Advisors subsidiary, reported selling 14,000 contracts worth nearly $2 billion—almost half of all futures sales by portfolio insurers on October 19, according to subsequent estimates of the Brady Commission. LOR Associates sold about $250 million worth in futures, then said they pulled back from the more massive liquidation their computer-based calculations suggested was in order; they later concluded that their caution, or general market chaos, had cost their clients $175 million that their system had been designed to protect. Another major portfolio insurer, Aetna, also reported "stepping out" of the market when cash-to-futures spreads became too wide.

The SEC Chairman Shouts Fire

In remarks that were made at 11 A.M. Eastern Daylight Time in response to questions after a speech, but were not reported until 1:04 P.M., Securities and Exchange Commission Chairman David Ruder (in only his third month on the job) stated: "There is a point at which I would be interested in talking with the New York Stock Exchange about a temporary, very temporary, halt in trading. I don't know at what point that is."[4] Princeton professor Sandy Grossman, speaking at the Annual Meeting of the American Eco-

---

[4]Quoted in "Black Monday: What Really Ignited the Market's Collapse After Its Long Climb," second in the series, "The Crash of '87," *The Wall Street Journal* (December 16, 1987), p. 20.

nomic Association in Chicago in late December 1987, at a session on the Crash of '87, likened this remark and another made by Ruder in early October, to the effect that the exchanges should be closed to "cool off" after 100-point moves, to announcing that the doors of a crowded theatre would be locked as soon as someone smelled smoke; it created enormous nervousness and incentives to rush to the exits, even if there were no fire.[5]

Fifteen minutes later, the SEC issued a statement denying that it was considering closing the markets, but the damage had already been done. Investors instructed their brokers to get them out at any price, and all semblance of market making collapsed. The Dow crossed the psychologically significant 2000 barrier about 1:45, rallied one last time for about 30 minutes beginning around 2:15, then headed into a free-fall, losing 250 points in the last 75 minutes of wild, hectic trading as it staggered to the final bell, closing at 1738.74. As investors' confidence in the market-making process collapsed, buyers and sellers became much more cautious about the credit-worthiness of their counterparts in each transaction, and this extra premium on solvency reduced market liquidity even further.

Surveying the Damage

Figure 5–3 and Tables 5–2 and 5–3 summarize the flow of transactions on the NYSE and CME on Black Monday. Trading was not only heavy; it was also concentrated among a surprisingly small number of institutions. Of the $21 billion in stock sales on all U.S. exchanges, $2.85 billion, or 14 percent, came from just four institutions; three were portfolio insurers (in all likelihood, Aetna, LOR Associates, and Wells Fargo), and one was a mutual fund company (Fidelity Investments). The top 15 sellers accounted for about 20 percent of total volume. On the buy side, concentration was a bit less, but still high: The 15 largest participants were responsible for 11 percent of total volume.

---

[5]Sanford Grossman, "Discussion of the Crash of '87" remarks delivered at the Annual Meeting of the American Economic Association, Chicago, December 29, 1987.

FIGURE 5–3

Equity Sales and Purchases, NYSE Stocks and CME Futures on Monday, October 19, 1987 (billions of dollars)

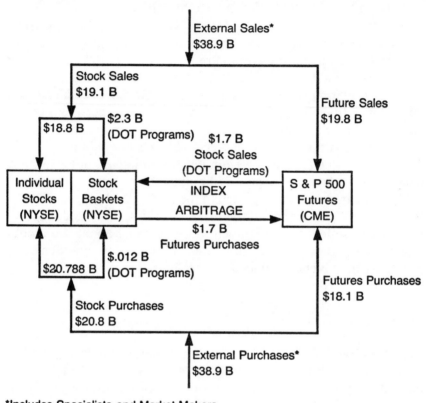

*Includes Specialists and Market Makers

Source: *Report of the Presidential Task Force on Market Mechanisms* (Washington: Government Printing Office, 1988), p. 35.

In the S&P 500 futures market, 162,000 contracts valued at $20 billion changed hands, as the price of a contract plunged by 29 percent. As might be expected, given the program trading strategies that linked the two markets, trading concentration was significant in futures, too; the 10 largest sellers accounted for fully 50 percent of non–market maker volume. Forty percent of non–market maker transactions, or $4 billion, were part of portfolio insurance schemes.

As the tide of selling swept over the stock market, the bond market began to turn around. Investors deduced that the carnage

TABLE 5–2
NYSE Large Institutional Dollar Volume (millions of dollars)

	October 15	October 16	October 19	October 20
Sales				
Portfolio Insurers	$ 257	$ 566	$1,748	$ 698
Other Pension	190	794	875	334
Trading-Oriented Investors	1,156	1,446	1,751	1,740
Mutual Funds	1,419	1,339	2,166	1,726
Other Financial	516	959	1,416	1,579
Total	3,538	5,104	7,598	6,077
Index Arbitrage (included above)	717	1,592	1,774	128
Purchases				
Portfolio Insurers	$ 201	$ 161	$ 449	$ 883
Other Pension	368	773	1,481	920
Trading-Oriented Investors	1,028	1,081	1,316	1,495
Mutual Funds	996	1,485	1,947	1,858
Other Financial	798	1,221	2,691	2,154
Total	3,391	4,721	7,884	7,290
Index Arbitrage (included above)	407	394	110	32

Source: *Report of the Presidential Task Force on Market Mechanisms* (Washington: Government Printing Office, 1988), p. 43.

on the stock exchange would trigger a sharp reversal of the Fed's recent policy of ever tighter money. By the close of bond trading, yields on 30-year Treasuries were down 31 basis points from the intraday peak of 10.45 percent, while three-month Treasury bill yields, reflecting a flight to quality, had declined to 6.22 percent from 6.81 percent.

At the market's close, the president's spokesman Marlin Fitzwater issued a statement expressing the president's "concern," his "view that the underlying economy remains sound," and his intention to "continue to closely monitor these developments." En route to board a helicopter to visit his wife Nancy, hospitalized for surgery after the discovery of breast cancer, Mr. Reagan commented, "I don't think anyone should panic, because all the economic indicators are solid." The media quickly checked the president's remarks against those of Herbert Hoover in 1929 and found

TABLE 5-3
CME Large Trader Volume (millions of dollars)

	October 14	October 15	October 16	October 19	October 20
			Sales		
Portfolio Insurers	$ 534	$ 968	$ 2,123	$ 4,037	$ 2,818
Arbitrageurs	108	407	392	129	31
Options	554	998	1,399	898	635
Locals	7,325	7,509	7,088	5,479	2,718
Other Pension	37	169	234	631	514
Trading-Oriented Investors	1,993	2,050	3,373	2,590	2,765
Foreign	398	442	479	494	329
Mutual Funds	46	3	11	19	40
Other Financial	49	109	247	525	303
Total Accounted for	11,045	12,666	15,347	14,801	10,152
Published Total	18,949	18,830	19,840	18,987	13,641
Percentage Accounted for	65.2	67.2	78.1	78.0	74.4
Portfolio Insurance as a Percentage of Publicly Accounted for Volume	14.4	18.8	25.7	43.3	37.9
			Purchases		
Portfolio Insurers	71	171	109	113	505
Arbitrageurs	1,313	717	1,705	1,582	119
Options	594	884	1,254	915	544
Locals	7,301	7,530	7,125	5,682	2,689
Other Pension	90	76	294	447	1,070
Trading-Oriented Investors	1,494	2,236	3,634	4,510	4,004
Foreign	240	298	443	609	418
Mutual Funds	0	27	73	143	51
Other Financial	155	57	126	320	517
Total Accounted for	11,259	11,976	14,763	14,320	9,915
Published Total	16,949	18,830	19,640	18,987	13,641
Percentage Accounted for	66.4	63.6	75.2	75.4	72.7
Portfolio Insurance as a Percentage of Publicly Accounted for Volume	1.8	3.9	1.4	1.3	7.0

Source: *Report of the Presidential Task Force on Market Mechanisms* (Washington: Government Printing Office, 1988), p. 44.

in them an eerily similar refrain about the sound and prosperous basis of production and business activity in the United States. It was a less-than-convincing reassurance.[6]

OCTOBER 20

When the New York exchange closed, it was 5 A.M. in Tokyo on Tuesday, October 20. When Tokyo investors awoke a few hours later, they rushed to liquidate their holdings, and the Nikkei 225 stock index experienced its largest one-day decline since the death of Joseph Stalin in 1953.

Despite the *tsunami* of selling pressure, the exchange itself was relatively calm, and volume in the morning session, at 100 million shares, was but one-tenth the daily average. The reason: the Tokyo Stock Exchange's rules call for a slowdown of trading if sellers outnumber buyers by 10 to 1 or more. As a result, trading occurred in the shares of only 55 of the 1,800 firms listed on the exchange. In the afternoon session, assisted by Finance Ministry–encouraged support buying by the four major securities firms (Daiwa, Nomura, Yamaichi and Nikko), volume picked up to 500 million shares. Still, the loss for the day as a whole was 14.9 percent, and would certainly have been more had market forces been given free rein. Indeed, in Singapore, where Nikkei 225 futures are traded, the December contract opened at 12000, plummeted to 5000, recovered to 22000, then closed breathlessly at 18100.

As Tokyo was shutting down, London was preparing to open. When it did, the non–blue chip stocks, which had withstood much of Monday's selling pressure, succumbed to the panic of Tuesday, and the market as a whole fell another 13 percent, for a two-day drubbing of 22 percent. The story in the rest of Asia and on the Continent was much the same: Sydney, off 25 percent; Frankfurt, .down 5 percent; Paris, off 6 percent; and Hong Kong, stocks and futures closed for the rest of the week. Sell orders raced the sun to be first in line to get out of stocks·

---

[6]Reported in the *New York Times* (October 20, 1987), p. D32.

Thirsting for Liquidity

Overnight in New York, the 50-odd specialist firms found themselves in a very unfamiliar situation. Normally their position at the epicenter of the market allowed them to profit handsomely from their superior access to public information. This time it had required them to take to their books a far larger inventory of stocks than they customarily held: about $1 billion. Stock exchange rules required that the stock be paid for five business days later, on October 26. As these firms contacted their bankers to borrow the necessary funds to finance their swollen inventories, even the best capitalized and most reputable among them found to their horror that the bankers considered themselves, as one delicately put it, "in no position to make commitments."[7]

Specialists weren't the only ones seeking credit; large securities firms, government securities dealers, risk arbitrageurs anticipating takeover action and now faced with margin calls—all were queueing up to the trough for more money, only to find that the spigot had slowed to a trickle. In the face of the quantum increase in economic uncertainty in the wake of Monday's crash, lenders were being much more particular as to whom they extended credit.

Frequently in the 19th century, financial panics had gripped one country after another. In 1873, after the 1866 collapse of Overend, Gurney & Company in London, Walter Bagehot, editor of the *Economist*, set out the theory of what to do to avoid the recessionary and even depressionary forces that followed such a collapse in financial confidence. Writing in his classic *Lombard Street*, Bagehot counseled having the central bank, the Bank of England, supplement its usual function of regulating the money supply by serving as a "lender of last resort." It should "discount in a crisis," extending credit by buying at a discount from face value the financial assets of institutions in trouble. By extending credit when no one else would, Bagehot saw that a central bank could provide the public good of confidence so essential to avoiding gridlock in the

---

[7]Quoted in "Terrible Tuesday: How the Stock Market Almost Disintegrated a Day after the Crash," *The Wall Street Journal* (November 20, 1987), p. 1.

financial markets and to promoting the resumption of normal levels of business activity.[8]

Bagehot's ideas had been instrumental in the establishment of the great central banks of Europe in the late nineteenth century and in the founding of the Federal Reserve System in 1913 in the wake of the Panic of 1907. In 1929, the Fed passed the test (barely) of stabilizing the markets in the period immediately after the Crash, though, as we shall see in Chapter 7, it was unable to make the correct decisions as the complex international economic situation deteriorated in the following four years.

The morning of October 20 was the moment of decision for Alan Greenspan, and he executed Bagehot's instructions perfectly. In a strikingly terse (given his somewhat loquacious pronouncements in the weeks leading up to the crash) statement released at 8:15 A.M., the Federal Reserve chairman stated: "The Federal Reserve affirms its readiness to serve as a source of liquidity to support the economic and financial system."[9]

As the Fed flooded the system with dollars by buying Treasury securities, driving short-term interest rates down dramatically, Gerry Corrigan, head of the Federal Reserve Bank of New York, personally telephoned the chairmen of the major money center banks and urged them to use the additional liquidity to meet the exploding demand for funds.

Hanging by a Thread

A large fraction of specialists' $3 billion total of buying power had been absorbed on Monday, so it was fortunate that buy-side, not sell-side, order imbalances kept some stocks from opening on Tuesday, October 20. By 10:30, encouraged by the Fed's aggressive, unconditional support of the banks and securities firms, the Dow was up nearly 200 points.

---

[8]See Charles P. Kindleberger, *Manias, Panics, and Crashes* (New York: Basic Books, 1978), pp. 163–165, for a good summary of Bagehot's ideas.

[9]Quoted in *Report of the Presidential Task Force on Market Mechanisms* (Washington: Government Printing Office, 1988), p. 52

One hour later, all the gain had been given up as the specialists and major brokerage firms took advantage of the temporary optimism in the market to unload their holdings of stocks. In the S&P 500 futures market, portfolio insurers had reappeared before 10 A.M., and futures again moved to a sizable discount to the cash market. Trading in blue chip stocks began to grind to a halt as sellers found no buyers and specialists were either out of liquidity or, fearing bankruptcy, chose not to use up the small amount of capital they had left. Sears stopped trading at 11:12, Eastman Kodak at 11:28, Philip Morris and IBM at 11:30, 3M at 11:31, and Dow Chemical at 11:43.

Rumors flashed across the trading floor that the CME clearinghouse was not financially viable (margin payments totaling $1.5 billion due two members were delayed), and again that SEC Chairman Ruder was going to close the exchange (in fact, only the president or the NYSE chairman had the authority to do so). Indeed, the Chicago Board Options Exchange (CBOE) later reported getting a call from the SEC around 11:30 Central Daylight Time to the effect that the NYSE was about to close.

On the AMEX, the specialist for the Major Market Index—a 20-stock index that, with 17 stocks also part of the Dow, had been created to mimic the Dow's action—ordered trading in MMI options to stop, citing a rule that required at least 80 percent of the stocks in the index to be trading for the options to trade. (An option is the right, but not the obligation, to buy or sell, during a specified time frame in the future, a single security or an entire index of securities at a price known today. It allows investors to limit their losses from a stock's price movements, while participating fully in gains.) The CBOE also closed, and after learning from Chairman John Phelan that the New York Stock Exchange was contemplating closing, CME Chairman Leo Melamed ordered, at 12:15, trading in the S&P 500 futures contract to stop.

Since 10:30, the futures contract discount to the cash market had been even larger than the 20 percent to 25 percent discounts reached during the closing hour on Black Monday. At noon, the discount was flirting with 40 percent, consistent with a Dow level of 1400 (see Figure 5–4). In part, this reflected the relatively "old" prices in the cash market index, where trading had been suspended for scores of stocks. Some investors, too, were not authorized to trade in futures and could not take advantage of the large discount.

FIGURE 5–4

S&P 500 Index and Futures Contract, and Portfolio Insurance Activity on Tuesday, October 20, 1987

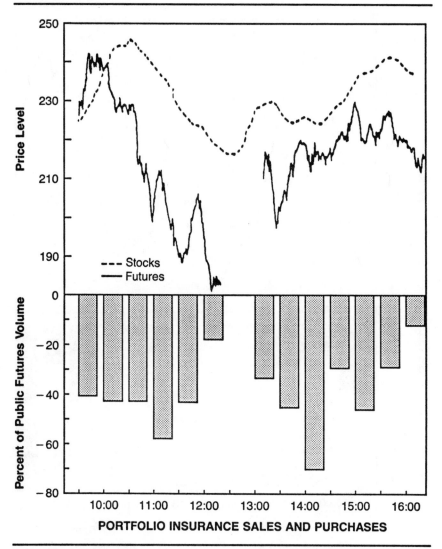

PORTFOLIO INSURANCE SALES AND PURCHASES

Source: *Report of the Presidential Task Force on Market Mechanisms* (Washington: Government Printing Office, 1988), p. 37.

FIGURE 5–5
Dow Jones Industrials One-Minute Chart, Index Arbitrage and Straight Program Activity on Tuesday, October 20, 1987

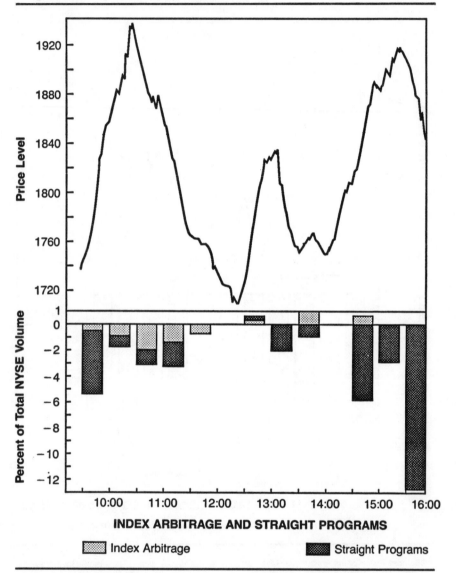

INDEX ARBITRAGE AND STRAIGHT PROGRAMS

▨ Index Arbitrage   ▨ Straight Programs

Source: *Report of the Presidential Task Force on Market Mechanisms* (Washington: Government Printing Office, 1988), p. 38.

More important, however, was the NYSE's prohibition of its broker dealers from using SuperDOT for index arbitrage transactions for their own account. With index arbitrage restricted by this proscription and by concerns over the CME's finances, fewer futures contracts were bought and the futures-to-cash price relationship was distorted. Stock prices expectations came to reflect the underpriced futures contracts, which served for some investors as a kind of beacon for the future value of the Dow. With stocks then appearing to be relatively dear, investors naturally sold them (see Figure 5–5).

(Less than Divine) Intervention

While the NYSE officials were meeting, a series of private and public actions were under way to stabilize the market. Gerry Corrigan was twisting the last of the reluctant arms at money center banks to get on with it and open the till; by 2 P.M., his work was done. A number of firms, under the prodding of their investment bankers and, many say, the administration, announced stock buyback plans to buoy the market. (It was rumored that these same investment bankers, still with huge inventories of securities that were rapidly dropping in price, were also pestering John Phelan to close the exchange.)

Finally, in a development that some battle-weary traders likened at the time to the parting of the Red Sea, a surge of buying hit the only futures index contract still open, the Chicago Board of Trade's Major Market Index futures contract. During the half-hour between 12:30 and 1 P.M., EDT, 808 contracts traded, representing an underlying value of about $60 million and a margin cost of substantially less (see Figure 5–6). Seventy percent of the trades were at low commission rates, an unusually high proportion. The contract went from a discount of over 50 percent to the cash market at 12:15 to a premium of over 10 percent by 12:50 (since many of the 20 stocks in the MMI weren't trading at the time, the actual premium was probably greater).

Almost immediately, stock index arbitrageurs sold the futures and bought the relatively cheap stocks, pulling the Dow up from a 12:15 low just above 1700 to over 1800 by 1 P.M. For an instant before the rebound, the blue chip index bottomed at 1616.21.

FIGURE 5–6
MMI Cash-to-Futures Spread, October 19 and 20, 1987

In points, at 15 minute intervals

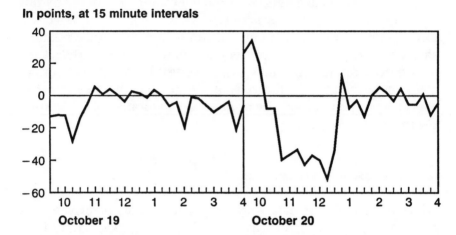

Source: *The Wall Street Journal* (November 20, 1987), p. 20.

Market manipulation? Perhaps. The CFTC stated in a report released on January 5 that it found no evidence of such, but independent observers and market participants raised questions about the agency's investigative methods and about the data submitted to the CFTC by the Merc; the Brady Commission's report also contained information that seemed to be at variance with the CFTC's analysis. Whatever the facts of the situation, John Phelan—who had commented at the close of business on Monday, "That's about as close to a meltdown as I'd ever want to see,"[10]—had been pushed even closer to the market's molten core by Tuesday's drama. Had the stock exchange closed (as it did during the Panic of 1873 and again at the start of the First World War), Phelan estimated it would have cost the Dow "another 800 to 1000 points," taking it back to the level in the depths of the 1981 and 1982 recessions.[11]

---

[10]Quoted in the *The Wall Street Journal* (October 20, 1987), p. 1.
[11]Quoted in Philip L. Zweig, "FW's Man of the Year: NYSE Chairman John Phelan," *Financial World* (December 29, 1987), p. 25.

The CME reopened the S&P 500 futures index at 1 P.M., though—unlike the MMI futures contract—it stayed well below the cash value of the S&P 500 for the rest of the day. With specialists reliquefied and more buy orders in the market, the Dow haltingly made its way back above 1900 by 3:30, then fell back—despite the SEC's convenient suspension of the prohibition on stock buy-backs in the last 30 minutes of trading—to finish the day with a 102-point gain. Trading volume had been 608 million shares, even more than Monday's crush, and decliners on the Big Board had outnumbered advancers by better than two to one. Still, the highly visible Dow had come back from its record loss with a record gain, in absolute points, one day later.

Thus ended the most turbulent week in the market's history since 1929. The Dow had lost 769 points, 31 percent of its value, in the first six days, amidst intense trading activity (see Table 5–4). On the last day, the entire market mechanism had been perilously close to a breakdown.

In this time of turbulence, the nation looked to the White House for something more than reassurances that the economy was fundamentally sound.

The First Steps

Later Tuesday afternoon, en route again by helicopter to visit with his wife, the president took the opportunity of an exchange with reporters to make a start. He announced that administration offi-

TABLE 5–4
Percentage of 1987 Daily Average Trading Volume, Various Exchanges, October 14 to October 20, 1987

	NYSE	NASDAQ	S&P 500	S&P Futures
October 14	115	97	135	162
October 15	143	107	153	180
October 16	188	131	166	133
October 19	335	149	199	72
October 20	337	189	156	42

Source: *Report of the Presidential Task Force on Market Mechanisms (Washington: Government Printing Office, 1988)*, p. 45.

cials would begin discussions with congressional leaders with a view toward producing a deficit-cutting budget. As the helicopter rotors were strategically turned on, the president appeared to say that he himself might take part in the discussions and that everything except Social Security was on the table. Reporters quickly conjectured that everything meant taxes and that the president may have signalled his willingness to accept a tax increase as part of a budget compromise.

Few commentators had fingered America's fiscal extravagance as the proximate cause for the market's tumble. But like accumulating cholesterol on the arterial walls before the onset of a heart attack, the federal budget deficit—and its contrast with the much more cautious spending and robust saving policies of Japan and Germany—was widely seen as a factor increasing the risks in the economic outlook: for the dollar, for interest rates, for real growth, and for stock prices.

Thus, the president's glacial change of attitude toward a tax increase was viewed as a very encouraging sign, particularly among foreign investors. On Wednesday, the Nikkei 225 stock index recovered more than half of Tuesday's decline, on volume of a more normal 1.1 billion shares, although the big four securities firms continued to support the market and margin requirements had been eased to encourage buying. The Bank of Japan had played a key role, injecting liquidity and calming fears of an interest rate increase.

London, too, came back sharply, by 6 percent, on October 21. In New York, 1749 of the 1935 issues advanced in Wednesday's rally, which boosted the Dow a record 187 points, to 2028, on volume of 449 million shares.

Despite the vigor of the October 21 rally, seasoned observers of market surges knew that a common pattern in other market upsets was for those investors who didn't get out during the market slide to sell into the first rally. They would not have long to wait to see that the Crash of '87 fit the pattern almost perfectly.

CHAPTER 6

AFTERSHOCKS

When traders arrived at their screens early on Thursday, October 22, they learned that Kuwait's main offshore oil terminal had been damaged seriously in a missile attack that both Kuwait and American officials attributed to Iran. Another Robert Prechter rumor was about, this time that in a communication with subscribers the previous evening he had announced that the market was headed for another big sell-off; the rumor later proved to be false. Foreign markets open at the time of the Middle East news took major hits—London was off 6 percent, Frankfurt 4 percent—and more foreign sell orders were on New York desks. Some of the stocks in the Dow again had trouble opening; by 10:15, nearly a quarter still had not done so. The feeling of déjà vu was very much in the air, and in early trading, the Dow was off 140 points.

HOLDING ON

Thursday's "down" did not turn into Monday's "out," however. Earlier in the day, the NYSE had asked several large market participants to refrain voluntarily from program trading activities; on Tuesday, the exchange had briefly, and unwisely, cut off access to its computers to limit such trading. While a voluntary restraint on program trading made some sense in the case of portfolio insurance, given the role of straight sell programs, a request to cease index arbitrage transactions risked decoupling the stock and stock index futures markets again and causing a repeat of the market instability that had occurred on October 19 and 20. Because portfolio insurance firms complied with the exchange's request, however, the market's initial decline on Thursday didn't trigger their powerful programmed "sell" strategies.

Citibank helped out, too, by trimming the prime by a quarter-point, to 9 percent, at the opening of the market. By midday, the market had stabilized, though sentiment was still negative as many investors who had not exited the market on Monday or Tuesday sought to do so now. The exchange brought some relief, to harried brokers at least, with its announcement that the market would close early, at 2 P.M., on Friday, Monday, and Tuesday, to allow firms to catch up on back-office paperwork. In the afternoon, the White House bolstered sentiment further with its statement that the president himself would meet with Democratic and Republican congressional leaders to discuss deficit-reduction steps. At the closing bell, the market was down 77, to 1950. The volume of 390 million shares brought the week's four-day total to over two billion shares—normally two weeks' worth.

Lights, Camera, Leadership?

In the wake of the 1929 Crash, Herbert Hoover had sought to bolster public confidence with a series of conferences with leaders from industry, the railroads, the utilities, construction firms, unions, and the farm sector. In the Depression, Franklin Roosevelt had used the "fireside chat." Ronald Reagan, naturally, turned to the medium of which he was master, television.

The president had navigated the shoals of leadership in response to the market crash quite cautiously, limiting his comments to brief remarks en route to visiting the first lady. Though even these had seemed disquietingly Hooveresque, it's unlikely that this president could have done much else, given the inherent unpredictability of the situation and his own unshakable belief in the correctness of the economic policies he had followed since 1981. Indeed, tragic as his wife's illness and operation had been, it did give him an extra measure of public indulgence for not speaking out more. The image of a husband visiting his hospitalized wife served, in a way that words would not have, to reassure the electorate that higher values than money were worth preserving and had been preserved.

On Thursday evening, however, the president agreed to hold a news conference, his first in seven months. Whatever the certainty of his own beliefs, foreign and domestic investors alike were convinced that the market's crash had been made much more likely by the misaligned economic policies of the United States, Japan, and Germany, and that the United States had failed to move toward closer alignment because of the president's refusal to countenance tax increases as a device to improve the balance of spending and saving in America.

At issue was leadership—the same issue that had dogged the White House since the loss of control of the Senate 11 months earlier, continuing through the Iran-Contra affair, the engagement in the Persian Gulf, and the recently scuttled Bork nomination. Now doubts had been raised about Ronald Reagan's capacity to lead the nation through the adjustments required in the post-Crash economic environment.

On everyone's lips and in everyone's mind was the question that began this narrative: "Can *It* happen again?" At this point, however, *it* referred not to the Crash but to the Depression that followed. Media commentators had interviewed many experts about the Depression, and they had made it clear to the electorate that several unwise decisions, by Herbert Hoover, by the leaderless Federal Reserve, by foreign officials, and by the Congress, had made the post-1929 slump much worse than it need have been. On October 22, political and economic leadership was at a premium, and Americans were not sure whether their 76-year-old president was up to the task.

What was certain as the news conference ended was that the president was up to playing his familiar role as the Great Communicator. Opening with a joke, referring to the crash as a "long-overdue correction," and mixing in an unexpected and favorable early report on the improvement in the budget deficit for the fiscal year just ended, the president was at the height of his game. He deftly neglected to mention that most of the deficit reduction was attributable to a one-time surge in capital gains tax realizations, the result of the Tax Reform Act of 1986.

President Reagan announced the appointment of the obligatory investigative commission, to be headed by investment banker and one-time senator from New Jersey Nicholas F. Brady, then handled questions about deficit adjustment and taxes with aplomb. Reiterating that everything except social security was on the table, the president criticized Congress, and particularly the Democrats, for failing to cut outlays. He still refused to disclose whether he would accept a tax increase of any kind, saying that congressional leaders would learn his negotiating position when the negotiating began.

Clearly, the president's strategy was to bargain for time; if the Crash turned out to have minimal effect on the economy, then he wouldn't have to concede on his principles. Students of the Depression recalled all too well how its depth was extended by overlong adherence to certain principles in the face of facts that suggested the application of others.

Foreigners, particularly, found the substance of Mr. Reagan's remarks distinctly less compelling than their style. In Friday trading in Tokyo, the Nikkei index suffered its second largest one-day decline, and the market was off 5 percent; Singapore and Sydney took larger plunges. London, too, started off down by about 5 percent, but then rebounded as it became evident that American investors found the president's remarks more palatable.

Indeed, domestic analysts and investors were even able to shake off Friday's disappointment that Secretary of State Shultz was unable to reach final agreement in Moscow with General Secretary Gorbachev on a missile treaty summit date. The Dow turned in a mixed session, closing a tumultuous week with a daily change of 0.33 points on volume of a more normal 246 million shares.

Days of Reckoning

As the Sunday papers turned to metaphysical reflections on the meaning of the Crash, Wall Street's denizens were busy preparing for the settlement days ahead, on Monday and Tuesday, October 26 and 27. Most of the financial fallout of the crash on the institutional side was thought to be known. First Options of Chicago had received an infusion of $200 million of capital from its parent, the recently beleaguered Continental Illinois. Several smaller specialists had been absorbed into larger firms, and though rumors had persisted about E. F. Hutton, the firm appeared ready to open for business. What was not known, however, was how individual investors were prepared to meet their margin calls.

Whatever this level of preparation, foreign investors made the issue moot by beginning the day with another massive wave of selling. In Tokyo, the Nikkei 225 index dropped another 4.7 percent, in the third worst decline in its history; the Hong Kong index, open for the first time in a week, plunged to a 33 percent lower level; London, too, slipped sharply, declining 6.7 percent.

With foreign and margin-related sales triggering the market, the Dow lost 4.5 percent in the first 30 minutes of trading, then slipped another 3.5 percent over the rest of the shortened trading day. It finished 8 percent below its Friday close, at 1794, on heavy volume—traded with eerie smoothness—of 309 million shares. During the day, in part to attempt to calm market nervousness, the NYSE announced that it would extend the early closing days from Tuesday through the end of the week. The Chicago Mercantile Exchange raised for the second time since the Crash the margins required for its S&P 500 contract, to $20,000 from a pre-crash $10,000 level. L. F. Rothschild & Company became the first brokerage firm to announce its losses in the Crash, $44 million, and to announce the layoffs to follow: 160 of its 2,000 employees. And in Florida, an investor shot and killed a Merrill Lynch broker, then took his own life.

Lender of Last Resort, Japanese Style

A few hours after the New York market concluded "Black and Blue Monday," the Ministry of Finance in Tokyo met with executives in charge of securities trading from Japan's three leading trust banks and three top life insurance companies, ostensibly to hold a "hearing" on the current market situation. The setting was similar to the meeting a week before with other stock market participants that had led to an October 21 rally that then spilled over to Europe and Wall Street. This time, the lead time was even shorter, as later Tuesday morning the Nikkei 225 index spurted on heavy buying, finishing the day up 2.7 percent and thereby gaining back more than half the ground lost on Monday.

Observers in Kabuto-cho, the stock exchange district in Tokyo, concluded that once again the Japanese *ringi* method of consensus decision making had produced the desired result. Ministry of Finance officials had asked whether the current market situation reflected economic fundamentals; securities market executives replied that they did not believe so. No more needed to be said; the fact that the government had asked the question told market participants the outcome the government found desirable—and they knew that, if they acted in accordance with the government's wishes, sufficient liquidity would be made available to them should they encounter financial difficulty.

To be sure, the government had more than just the broad public interest in mind. In November, it planned to auction two million shares of the recently privatized Nippon Telephone & Telegraph and was counting on the revenue to allow it to take some of the fiscal stimulus measures other nations were demanding.

The Tokyo recovery was matched in Hong Kong, where the announcement of the doubling, to $4 billion, of a government safety net for the market triggered a 6.4 percent rise in the Hang Seng index. Buoyed by the rebound in Asian markets, European exchanges surged as well. London's recovery was more uncertain than most, as investors awaited the government's decision whether to proceed with a scheduled offering of British Petroleum shares. In New York, news of firmer prices abroad triggered a strong 52-point, 2.9 percent rebound in the blue-chip Dow, though broader market indexes were more mixed. Thanks to a peculiarly Japanese version of the lender-of-last-resort function and to the same globalization of capital markets that amplified the magnitude of the stock market decline, a "crash after the Crash" had been, for the moment, averted.

THE DOLLAR TAKES OVER

As the market found its footing, the much-ballyhooed "budget summit" talks between the president, his staff, and congressional leaders moved past the ceremonial stage. It quickly became apparent that the White House intended to give ground very gradually on the tax side, agreeing only to the most minor of "revenue enhancements." The revamped Gramm-Rudman deficit reduction law required agreement on a minimum of $23 billion in tax hikes or spending cuts for the current fiscal year by November 20, and it quickly became clear that no consensus existed that would allow more dramatic action to be taken.

Though foreign central banks joined the Fed in pumping liquidity into the system to counter the impact of the crash, there had been little indication that they were ready to make a dramatic move, such as a discount rate cut, in the direction of easier money and thus stronger domestic economic growth. With initial hopes of quick progress in realigning fiscal policies stymied by the glacial pace of American budget talks (and foreign intransigencies), the markets quickly concluded that the only route to an early resolution of the imbalances between the deficit American and surplus Japanese and German economies lay in further dollar depreciation. By week's end, the U.S. currency had been marked down against its Japanese and German counterparts to 40- and 7-year lows, respectively. Traders concluded the Fed had had the choice between defending the dollar (and pushing interest rates up) and defending the economy, and had chosen the latter (see Figure 6–1).

Wealth Effects and Post-Louvre Bands

The Fed's latitude to take this course of action, when a month before it had done just the opposite, rested on two developments. The Crash had reduced the market value of the economy's assets by roughly $1 trillion, though rising bond prices as interest rates fell provided some offset. According to the research that had won the Nobel Prize for Franco Modigliani of M.I.T., this reduction in wealth would have an impact on consumer spending, slowing it down by about $5 for every $100 decline in asset values, or $50 billion in all. To some analysts, the rapid runup in the market in 1987 meant that consumers hadn't come to count on all their paper profits in making spending decisions, so in their view this estimate was too high. Still, there was general agreement that by slowing household outlays the Crash had, for the moment, reduced substantially the risk of inflation that had so bothered financial markets to mid-October.

Thus, though the dollar's renewed decline would be somewhat inflationary, investors figured that in the post-Crash economy enough slack capacity would be available to absorb increased demand (from

FIGURE 6–1
The Dollar after the Crash

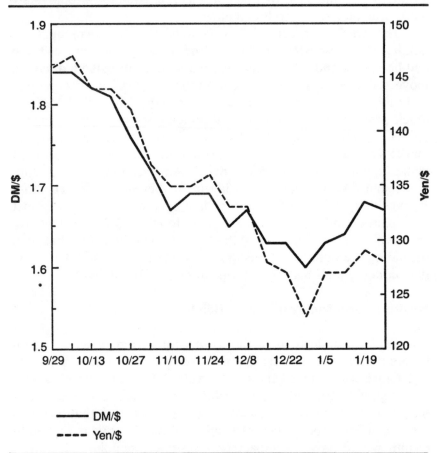

Source: Data are from *The Economist,* various issues.

Americans and foreigners alike) for now-still-cheaper American goods and services. This expected increase in available production capacity as a result of the Crash also argued against any hike in interest rates because that would only slash spending and employment further.

The second reason the Fed was able to allow the dollar to slide, particularly against the mark, is that in their October 19 kiss-

and-make-up session Treasury Secretary Baker and Finance Minister Stoltenberg had secretly agreed on new, post-Louvre Agreement ranges for the dollar against the mark. These new undercover bands defused the pre-Crash conflict between the North American and European economic leaders, giving each more latitude to pursue policies focused on the needs of their domestic economies, as they saw them.

Spooking Foreign Capital

To be sure, this path-of-least-resistance route was not without its risks. As foreign investors saw the dollar headed south, they might dump American stocks and bonds in order to avoid capital losses on their investments. To avoid this, in the week following the Crash, German authorities made sure that they pumped sufficient liquidity into their financial system to hold the German-U.S. interest rate differential at a level consistent with dollar stability.

After the stock market stabilization on October 27 and as currency traders concluded that no dramatic monetary or fiscal policy moves were in the offing, the Bundesbank, the Fed, and the Bank of Japan let the dollar decline, seeking only to intervene to keep its fall orderly to minimize the risk of foreign investor bailout. After all, they reasoned, once the U.S. currency did touch bottom, American assets would be quite cheap, especially if the risk of capital loss was gone, and what had been a vicious cycle could turn into a virtuous one.

The immediate effect of the dollar's fall was very positive for American stocks. On Thursday, October 29, the Dow posted its third best absolute point gain ever, rising 91.5 points to 1938. On Friday, the advance continued, helped by news of a December 7 missile treaty summit in Washington, as the Dow rose another 55 points.

In London, the government's decision to press ahead with the offering of $12.3 billion of British Petroleum shares was greeted with trepidation, but the inclusion of a buy-back feature by the Bank of England seemed to mollify investors. Four American investment banking firms, however, Goldman Sachs, Shearson Lehman, Morgan Stanley, and Salomon Brothers, stood to lose as much as $600 million because the deal went forward.

The following Monday, a fortnight after the crash, the recovery broadened as trading volume receded to more customary levels, though trading hours also returned to normal, and the Dow closed at 2014, its highest level in 12 days. Reflecting the perception that the initial crisis in the financial system had passed, investors began sacrificing the safety of Treasury securities for higher yields elsewhere, and the three-month Treasury bill rate rose by half a percentage point, to 5.8 percent.

NEGOTIATED SETTLEMENTS

With the market situation more stable, attention turned to the longer range consequences of the Crash. Economic policymakers, realizing there was a limit to how much dollar depreciation the world's equity markets could take, returned to their task of adjusting monetary and fiscal policy levers in Germany, Japan, and the United States. Regulators in several countries bent to their task of diagnosing the "market break," as the Brady Commission staff came to call it, and recommending changes in market procedures. Industrial companies worldwide tried to assess just how much weaker a post-Crash economy would be; Porsche decided immediately to cut production. Takeovers on the drawing boards were shelved indefinitely; others were activated. Wall Street began preparing the dismissal notices necessary to streamline an industry facing reduced income prospects.

Few firms had been spared from the carnage of October. Highflier discount brokerage firm Charles Schwab, the darling of the Street in September when it went public, suffered a $22 million trading loss when Hong Kong real estate magnate Teh Huei Wang was unable to meet $84 million in margin calls on October 19. Dean Witter fired about half of its municipal bond staff, then hired some of those discharged by Salomon the month before when it got out of the business. E. F. Hutton was soon to be forced into the arms of Shearson, its suitor (at much higher prices) of a year before.

Good Will Gestures

On November 5, with the dollar's decline gathering momentum, German monetary authorities agreed to lower their securities repurchase rate to its midsummer level of 3.5 percent, and to cut the Lombard rate, the charge on supplementary borrowings from the Bundesbank, one-half point to 4.5 percent. Almost simultaneously, commercial banks in the United States lowered their prime rate a quarter-point, to 8.75 percent. These developments restored some of the lustre to Treasury Secretary Baker's bull-in-a-china-shop reputation won in the mid-October spat with the German Finance Minister and improved the outlook for post-Crash economic growth.

The White House chose the same time to announce the easing of a portion of the remaining $250 million in trade sanctions imposed in the spring against the Japanese for violations of a semiconductor pricing agreement. According to U.S. findings, the Japanese were no longer setting unfairly low prices for their goods in third-country markets. This distinctly antiprotectionist move was designed to improve the atmospherics for continued international economic policy cooperation in the weeks ahead. It also was a gesture of appreciation to the Japanese, and in particular to the new prime minister, Noburu Takeshita, who had taken office November 1, for letting the dollar fall against the yen in recent weeks.

Tax Hike in a Recession?

As the budget summit negotiations dragged on, it was clear that the United States was going to need all the good will it could muster from its trading partners. With the relative stabilization of the stock market, the impetus to make sweeping concessions in the budget negotiations disappeared for both sides, just as Reagan strategists had hoped it would.

Indeed, for many it seemed wrongheaded for the government to be considering an increase in taxes or a reduction in outlays with the economy perhaps facing a recession or worse. Hadn't that been what was learned from the teachings of John Maynard Keynes? However discredited his ideas had become in the environment of postwar prosperity, weren't they just what the doctor ordered in times of incipient depression? Hadn't Herbert Hoover's 1932 tax increase actually made the Depression worse?

To be sure, there were those who hoped action to reduce federal budget deficits would be minimal; they ranged across the ideological spectrum. Northwestern's Robert Eisner, a dyed-in-the-wool Keynesian, thought that, worldwide, fiscal policy was already too tight and that any American moves to rein in government outlays or increase taxes would not be matched by equivalent expansionary initiatives in Germany or Japan. More conservative economist Larry Kotlikoff of Boston University advised to "forget about the deficits," on the grounds that they were misleading indicators of the stance of fiscal policy, and that they in particular failed to measure the impact of expected *future* fiscal policy initiatives on spending decisions. Kotlikoff, too, thought fiscal policy was already too tight, because of the future social security tax hikes scheduled for the mid-1990s.[1]

Why Worry about Deficits?

The mainstream of professional opinion, however, agreed that out-of-control federal deficits were at the root of the trade-imbalance problem that signaled policy misalignment in the global economy. A country's payments imbalance with other countries is the mirror image of its balance of national income (which is, as a matter of accounting, equal to national production) and spending. If a country spends beyond its income, it must import the difference, borrowing from abroad to finance the foreign purchases. If its income exceeds its expenditures, the goods not bought at home are available for export.

The key here is the balance of *national* income and spending—in other words, national saving. The Japanese government also runs large budget deficits; that is, the government buys more Japanese goods and services than it can pay for with taxes. But households and corporations in Japan earn a great deal more than they spend, so they have plenty left over to finance the Japanese government shortfall *and* loan money to foreigners to finance their purchases of Japanese exports. That is, when considering the expenditures of the Japanese public and private sector together, they are still less than the production performed and income (wages, profits, and taxes) earned by those sectors; the Japanese nation is a net saver.

[1] See for example Kotlikoff's "Forget About the Deficits," the *New York Times* (November 2, 1987), p. A24, and my response in a letter to the editor, the *New York Times* (November 18, 1987), p. A24.

Thus, the Japanese have goods left over to export to foreigners and money left over to finance the purchases. In contrast, since their public sector absorbs all of America's private sector saving and then some, Americans must import the extra goods and services they want to buy, and borrow to pay for them.

In principle, there is nothing wrong with taking on debt, as long as the proceeds are used wisely. If they are, when it comes time to repay the loan, resources will be available to do so. But most observers have felt the United States has been borrowing from abroad either for consumption, in the form of social security payments to the middle class, or to finance its huge military expenditures, thereby providing insurance—no one knows whether too much or too little—for the entire Western alliance.

Under these circumstances, it is questionable whether America will be able to make payment (i.e., generate the necessary export surpluses) in a way that will be politically acceptable to the current generation, whose standard of living will have to fall—no one knows how much—to accommodate the transfer of resources abroad. The mainstream of the profession thinks it advisable to reduce the growth of foreign borrowing (i.e., reduce the deficit in trade with other countries) now in order to allow for a smoother process of servicing the debt in the future.

A Delicate Task

The art in this budget summit exercise, then, heeding Keynes, was not to cut outlays or increase taxes too much in the near term. That would in fact add deflationary pressure to an already-weak economy. Rather, what was needed was a *credible, multiyear* program of federal deficit reduction. Experience with the 1981 Economic Recovery Tax Act—itself an example of a credible (in the sense that Congress was not about to repeal it), multiyear program of deficit expansion—suggested that the mere announcement of the program had raised long-term interest rates and crowded out business fixed investment before the tax cuts even had time to take effect. In the jargon of economics, the "multiplier," or "ripple effect," of a tax cut could initially be negative. Reasoning symmetrically, the implementation of a credible, multiyear program of deficit reduction to meet the economy's long-term needs would do little harm to the economy in the short run and might well actually lower long-term interest rates, and thus "crowd in" investment and support an economy on the brink of recession or worse.

BIRTH OF A MOUSE

For all the agreement among economists about the right course of action, the politicians were having their usual difficult time of reaching an accord. After all, an election, and a presidential one at that, was only 12 months away.

Over the weekend of November 7 and 8, confusion and acrimony developed about who had said what at the bargaining table. Word of this new conflict, coupled with the embarrassing withdrawal of the president's second Supreme Court nominee, former marijuana smoker and Harvard professor Douglas Ginsberg, was followed by a 3 percent plunge in the Dow on Monday, November 9.

Over the next two weeks, brinksmanship was the order of the day as, abetted by some mixed signals from the White House, the dollar's fall became disorderly. German pressure increased for an agreement to reduce the budget deficit as the *quid pro quo* for their earlier reduction of interest rates. The September trade deficit report, released on November 12, took some of the heat off, since it showed a surprisingly strong $1.6 billion improvement from August, to a shortfall of $14.08 billion.

Six days later, the release of a highly critical congressional report on the Iran-Contra affair revived anew questions about the president's leadership. Concerns about the strength of the post-Crash economy also were raised again by the release of October housing starts, which were reported as off 8 percent, to a four-year low, reflecting the rise in mortgage interest rates that had preceded the crash.

With members of his own party increasingly disaffected with the composition of the budget package taking shape, the president decided to turn up the heat a bit further by ordering the $23 billion of Gramm-Rudman cuts in outlays to go into effect on schedule November 20. These cuts weighed more heavily on the military budget than did the package being discussed by congressional negotiators.

Finally, on the last possible day, conferees agreed to a two-year, $76 billion list of tax increases and outlay reductions. Of the $30 billion in listed first-year savings, $11 billion came from tax increases, $12.8 billion from reductions in outlays, and another $6.4 billion from asset sales and other one-time devices. But these figures only represented an outline of intentions; after the Thanksgiving recess, the Congress was to return to "fill in the blanks." When that tortuous process was completed, the Gramm-Rudman cuts would be rescinded.

Market response to the budget summit effort was uniformly negative: Senator Packwood dubbed it a "miserable pittance," while the *Economist* reported, "After a horribly protracted labor, Washington's bargainers over the budget gave birth to their mouse on November 20."[2] Foreign finance ministers came forward with statements of official approval and support. But investors, convinced that if put to the test the American political process, as currently populated, could not take decisive action, decided to vote with their money against U.S. equities and the U.S. currency.

Back to Square One

In part to slow the pace of the dollar's fall and to demonstrate their official support for Washington's meager effort, the Bundesbank on November 24 led a coordinated Continental wave of interest rate reductions by lowering its securities repurchase rate another quarter-point. And on December 1, the German authorities announced a plan to stimulate capital spending, involving financing at concessionary rates for DM 21 billion worth of projects. Still, noting that the actual government outlays for these projects would run into the millions, not billions, of marks, analysts concluded that Washington's mouse had a German cousin.

As a result of these disappointments, the U.S. sell-off accelerated in the week after Thanksgiving, and at the close of trading on Friday, December 4, the Dow Jones industrials index stood at 1767, down 144 points for the week, a full 12.3 percent below its close on the first trading day of November and a slim 1.7 percent

---

[2]Quoted in the *The Economist* (November 29, 1987), p. 12.

above the October 19 trough. Using the broadest market index, that of Wilshire Associates, the value of American equities had declined by $100 billion since the day of the crash and, at $2.2 trillion, was a full one-third below its level on August 25, at the peak of the bull market.

During this time, the dollar had lost more than 7 percent of its value against the German mark, going from 1.80 on October 16 to 1.67. Vis-à-vis the yen, the U.S. currency stood at 142.5 in mid-October, then slipped to 132 in early December. Such is the magnitude of the vacuum created by the absence of policy coordination.

OPEC and Gorbachev Help Out

With Mikhail Gorbachev in Washington and news of renewed conflict at OPEC's year-end meeting, stocks rebounded smartly in the first three days of December's second week. Optimistic assessments by economists and other business-cycle watchers about the effect of the Crash on spending decisions also helped; they recalled that the purchasing managers' report and the employment release, both issued in December's first week, had indicated only a very modest effect of Black Monday on purchasing and hiring decisions.

On Thursday, December 10, however, the release of the U.S. trade deficit for October showed an astonishing $17.6 billion shortfall, a full 25 percent worse than September's $14.1 imbalance. Most analysts had expected a repeat of the September performance.

In response, the Dow fell 49 points in the first 15 minutes of trading. After that it stabilized, however, as traders learned that the Federal Reserve had stood aside to permit another discrete downward adjustment in the dollar's value, to levels not seen in 40 years: 129 yen and 1.64 marks. On Friday, December 11, the market picked itself back up as the dollar continued to come under heavy selling pressure; the Dow finished at 1867. The week's gain—100 points—was the largest in absolute terms ever and, at 5.5 percent, a record in percentage terms as well.

The market had weathered an important test. Brokers fearing a year-end sell-off for tax purposes rested a little easier, as did those who thought pension funds might engage in a wholesale dumping of stocks for bonds.

For the next three trading days, the Dow continued its upward trek, buoyed by a conclusion to the OPEC meeting that sent oil prices tumbling by $2.50, or nearly 15 percent. As one oil minister put it, the Iran-Iraq war, and the runaway production and discounting its revenue requirements caused, had "taken a fourteenth seat among the thirteen members" of OPEC.[3] The benefit to the inflation outlook implied by the oil-price collapse nicely complemented reports on economic activity in November—on industrial production, capacity utilization (at a three-year high), and housing (a bounce-back from October's depressed levels)—suggesting that the initial impact of the Crash had not been as catastrophic as feared. As frosting on the market's cake, House conferees negotiating the specifics of the budget accord agreed, on December 16, to drop all attempts to tax takeovers. The Dow gained 20 points in the last hour and closed at 1974, 207 points above its December 4 low.

As the holidays approached, budget summiteers scrambled to find all the revenue enhancements and expenditure cuts required to breathe life into the mouse created on November 20. In the wee hours of December 22, Congress forwarded to the president the required implementing legislation. Adjusted for one-time savings and accounting gimmicks, the accord reduced the expected budget deficit for fiscal year 1988 by $23 billion (the same size as the Gramm-Rudman target it superseded); fiscal 1989 savings were several billion higher.

LOUVRE BY PHONE

Later on the day the president signed this bill, the Group of Seven issued a communique stating their belief that over the past two months the dollar had fallen far enough and that "excessive fluctuations" in exchange rates from this point onward could damage the outlook for world economic growth. The announcement, which had been negotiated by telephone in the month since Washington agreed on a budget deficit-reduction plan, was a substitute for a

---

[3]Quoted in the *New York Times* (December 17, 1987), p. D1.

formal gathering of the finance ministers from the major industrial countries. It represented, in effect, an attempt to reinstitute a Louvre Accord–style understanding to follow on the monetary and fiscal policy adjustments made in the wake of the market's crash. Though the text of the communique was less clear than the Louvre Accord had been on the issue of acceptable trading ranges for the dollar against the mark, yen, and other currencies, most currency analysts thought that the December 23 pronouncement did commit the central banking fraternity to defend a revised band of exchange rates for the dollar.

Currency dealers had little faith that the policy adjustments made since the crash implied that current exchange rates were necessarily equilibrium rates, and they quickly went about testing the resolve of the authorities. In the thin trading that characterizes year-end markets, the dollar's value was driven down by almost another 5 percent, to 121 yen and 1.57 marks. The continued instability in currency markets contributed to year-end selling in the stock markets in Tokyo, London, and New York. In the last, the publication of the index of leading economic indicators for November also had an impact; as feared, driven by the stock market's collapse, it declined more sharply than it had in 3 1/2 years, falling 1.7 percent. The Dow closed out 1987 at 1939, up 2.3 percent on a year-end 1986 that seemed a very long time ago.

Squeezing the Shorts

Central banks expected demand for dollars to rise in the early days of 1988, as corporate treasurers who had postponed booking earnings from strong currency countries for tax purposes got on with their business. At the opening of business on Monday, January 4, central banks let it be known that they would be in the market aggressively to counter any more downward pressure on the dollar from short-sellers—suggesting that the lower limits of the trading ranges agreed to in the December 23 statement were 120 yen/dollar and 1.55 marks/dollar.

As the week unfolded and the dollar started to rebound from its late-1987 lows, the Bundesbank, the Bank of Japan, and even the Federal Reserve Bank bought dollars aggressively. The action of buying while the dollar was on the rise—essentially a portfolio-insurance-in-reverse strategy—had the same effect on the upside in currencies as the real thing had had in the stock market. By Thursday, January 7, the dollar had appreciated by 7 percent against the yen, moving to 130 yen/dollar, while the mark was back at 1.66, also a 7 percent–plus rise. Investors in the world's stock markets were much impressed by the central banks' cunning in intervening in currency markets, as they were by the publication of several economic reports that suggested that in December economic activity had shown further resilience. Heavy discounting had moved Christmas merchandise, auto sales in December had rebounded from October and November lows, and the purchasing managers' survey showed a rebound in activity to pre-Crash levels. By the close of trading Thursday, January 7, the Dow had spurted to 2052, a rise of 113 points in a calendar week's time. To market professionals who had come to wonder if all the rules of the game for stock price movements had changed, the appearance of what seemed to be a typical January effect rally was comforting indeed.

Twenty-four hours later, on the day the Brady Commission issued its report on what it euphemistically called the "market break," the Dow stood at 1911, having lost 141 points, or 6.85 percent of its value, in one day.

CHAPTER 7

À LA RECHERCHE DU
TEMPS PERDU

The suddenness of the market's free-fall quickly conjured up all of the old nightmares. The initial softness in the stock market on Friday, January 8, had been in response to stronger-than-expected employment data for December. Most economists had been expecting a rise in the unemployment rate; instead, it fell. When robust employment increases were reported, they implied that solid advances in industrial production would be reported for December the following Friday; quickening production meant sharper growth in incomes, a faster pace for spending, more inflationary pressure, and thus higher interest rates. The dollar's sharp fall also looked to start showing up at the producer price level, and oil prices had firmed in the wake of cold weather in the United States and supply problems in Europe.

Compounding investors' concerns over inflation were fears that the current dollar support ranges simply were not sustainable in light of the relatively modest policy adjustments that had taken place since the crash. The market feared the release of the trade deficit figures for November a week hence; rumor had it that since these would be the first trade data to reflect the collapse of the dollar after the crash, "J-curve" effects would balloon the import totals. If the trade deficit were disappointing, the dollar would come under attack, inflation fears would heat up further, interest rates would rise, and stocks would dive.

It all sounded very much like a rerun of the October 14 through October 19 fire drill, and investors were very quick on Friday to reduce their exposure. Once the market headed down, portfolio insurance programs kicked in, and—as if to illustrate the perils outlined in the Brady report—interacted with stock index arbitrage transactions to produce a late-afternoon free-fall in the Dow.

"A Repeat of Black Monday?" was the lead story on most newscasts over the weekend. Though most analysts were able to find some significant differences between October 16 and January 8 fairly quickly (Friday's volume had been thin due to a storm; and cooperation, not confrontation, was the watchword among the Group of Seven), a feeling of nervousness remained, and the opening of the Tokyo market Sunday evening was awaited with a mixture of fear and anticipation.

As it happened, stocks rose on January 11, and the November trade data released the following Friday revealed a substantial improvement, to a shortfall of only $13.2 billion. It was no coincidence, however, that on Thursday the NYSE requested major firms to refrain from portfolio insurance activity for the next six days if the Dow fell or rose by 75 points. The events of January 8 had demonstrated that, whatever the data suggested about the economy's recovery, investors—and exchange officials themselves—were still very jumpy, and very nervous.

LOOKING OVER OUR SHOULDERS

In the wake of Black Monday, the Proustian fascination with Black Thursday, Monday, and Tuesday (October 24, 28, and 29, 1929) and their aftermath grew and grew. The *New York Times* had taken to running a comparison, reproduced on the following page, of the market's performance in the days after the 1929 crash and the days after the 1987 "market break." The two lines tracked each other quite closely through the 45-day mark, though in 1929 stocks plunged far longer before rebounding to stand in much the same relation to the pre-Crash level of share prices as the Dow did at year-end 1987 (Figure 7–1).

As suggested in Chapter 1, the structural characteristics of the U.S. and international economies in the 1920s and 1980s contained some telling similarities: the ethic of markets relatively free of regulation; the explosion of debt, both domestically and internationally, and the emergence of workout problems in the commodity sectors and in foreign loans; and the changing of the guard of

FIGURE 7–1
The Dow Jones Industrials Index, 1987 versus 1929

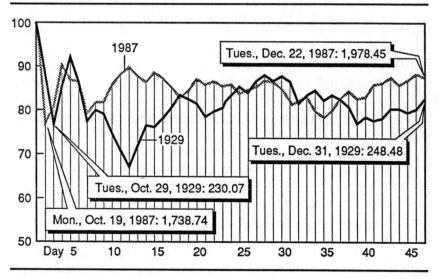

Source: *New York Times* (December 27, 1987).

national economic competitiveness, with all that implied for the instability of exchange rates and interest rates, and for the rise of protectionist sentiment. Equally important for the direct comparison of the two crashes, however, and for an assessment of whether and when the other shoe of depression will drop in 1988 or beyond, are the states of national economies and the interrelationships of national capital markets in the weeks and months leading up to the market collapses.

The "Business Cycle Bonus"

Chroniclers of the aftermath of the Crash of 1987 have taken much comfort from the fact that the American economy had peaked before the Crash of 1929, whereas that was not the case in October of 1987. Indeed, the reference peak for the 1920s expansion according to the National Bureau of Economic Research is June 1929, and in the three months thereafter, industrial production declined at an annual rate of 15 percent. Auto production in September of

1929 was but 415,000, compared with 622,000 in March.[1] In contrast, in the third quarter of 1987, industrial production increased at an annual pace of nearly 6 percent. This additional momentum unquestionably has helped the economy absorb the shock of the collapse in share values. But in assessing our economic prospects in the coming months and years, it's wise to recall that even after the 1929 catastrophe the economy seemed to stabilize during the early months of 1930, before, as Joseph Schumpeter put it, "People felt the ground give way beneath their feet."[2] If, in tracing the course of other events that preceded and followed the 1929 Crash, we detect a disturbingly familiar, and in all likelihood unavoidable, pattern, then all the "business cycle bonus" may buy us is more time until a depression sets in.

A Political Cycle Reprieve or Sentence?

Another factor that may provide extra time to wait for the other shoe to drop (to get our affairs in order or to put them in greater disorder) is the difference in the electoral cycle between 1929 and 1987. The Crash of 1929 occurred after an election year, and since presidents at that time took office on March 4, this was slightly less than eight months after Herbert Hoover moved into the White House. The economy's dynamics in 1929 and thereafter reflected in part campaign promises and initiatives that were the will of a new president.

In 1988, of course, the nation is in the process of choosing the next occupant of the White House. Consequently, as many have observed, the Federal Reserve will be more likely to err on the side of monetary ease as long as it can afford to do so, based on concerns about the dollar and inflation. Any policy initiatives, however, such as the budget summit accord, that have been taken in the fiscal realm to contain the crisis will have little momentum or long-run credibility.

---

[1]Quoted in Charles P. Kindleberger, *The World in Depression, 1929–39* (Berkeley: University of California Press, 1973), p. 117.

[2]Ibid., p. 137.

Memories of William Jennings Bryan

Indeed, economic policy issues are at the center of the 1988 political campaign. As David Hale has observed, this is the first political campaign to be undertaken since 1896 in which the United States was a debtor nation.[3] In Hale's view, the proper analogy is not so much between the Crash of 1929 and the Crash of 1987 as it is between the Panic of 1893 and 1987's "Market Break."

In the 1893 episode, growing enthusiasm of the United States for an experiment with a bimetallic (i.e., silver and gold) monetary standard—the result of disenchantment with the deflation and hard times brought about by the country's return to gold after the Civil War—led British capital to flee New York. It had done the same in 1890, when the British investment bank Baring Brothers came close to collapse because of a default problem on Argentine bonds; the United States, as another developing nation (one might even say, another "newly industrializing country") in the Americas, suffered by association.

The withdrawal of British capital produced higher interest rates and a 40 percent decline in stock market values, and sent shocks throughout the nation's financial system. Stability was restored only when the federal government secured a loan from a consortium of American and British banks, but the dependence of the country's fortunes on foreign capital aroused much populist hostility. This found voice in William Jennings Bryan, who as the Democratic presidential nominee in the election of 1896 reversed his party's traditional support of the gold standard and denounced the servile position vis-à-vis London it forced on the United States. As the campaign unfolded and Bryan's rhetoric became hotter, the stock market gave up all its gains since the 1893 crash and U.S.-British interest rate differentials rose steadily. With William McKinley's election, foreign capital flowed back in, and subsequent gold discoveries in South Africa and the Yukon made the monetary-standard issue moot by the turn of the century.

---

[3]David D. Hale, "Is the Stock Market Crash of 1987 Comparable to 1929 or 1893? or Will There Be a New Jazz Age Before the Next Depression?" Remarks to the National Business Economics Issues Council, November 1987.

To be sure, the America of the late 1980s is in a far different position in the world economy than the America of the late 1890s was, debtor status or no. It is larger, and it provides a military shield for the Western alliance. Nevertheless, populists of the left (e.g., Richard Gephardt and Jesse Jackson) and right (e.g., Jack Kemp) have at times been in active contention in the presidential sweepstakes, and it is not inconceivable that they, or their influence on party platforms or the positions of party nominees, could upset foreign owners of capital as November 8, 1988, draws nigh.

The Foreign Electoral Cycle

Foreign investors also will pay close attention to the content and sustainability of economic policies pursued in their countries. In Germany, the German government of Helmut Kohl was returned to power in the elections of January 1987. In the United Kingdom, Margaret Thatcher won a third term in June. Though the French must hold elections in 1988, and the Italians are as usual careening from crisis to crisis, the political environment in Europe as a whole is characterized more by continuity than change. This increases the credibility of any policy actions taken, while at the same time making a change of course, if one is required for technical economic reasons, less necessary on political grounds.

In Japan, however, Noburu Takeshita assumed leadership only a few days after the crash. Though his party, the Liberal Democrats, has been in power for the entire postwar period, Mr. Takeshita is cut from rather different, more inward-looking cloth than his more internationally-oriented predecessor, Yasuhiro Nakasone. As the leader of the nation moving to the center of today's global economic stage, Mr. Takeshita is in a somewhat analogous situation to that occupied by Herbert Hoover in 1929. The comparison is not completely tight, of course, since domestic demand in the Japanese economy was on an upward track in October 1987, and as this is written, the Japanese stock market has proven far more resilient than Wall Street and London have been in 1988, or than Wall Street was in 1929.

On the other hand, though, neither had Wall Street crashed when Hoover moved into the White House; perhaps the most interesting form of this analogy matches October 1987 in Japan with February 1929 in the United States. On this reading, perhaps the crash in Japan is yet to come. Before addressing that very pregnant topic, however, let us explore more fully the patterns of similarity between 1929 and 1987.

1929 REVISITED[4]

Indeed, at the time of the U.S. crash in 1929, most other stock markets already had peaked. The mid-1920s bubble in Germany had burst in 1927, London had topped out in January 1929, and Paris in February. Wall Street's walking recovery in stock prices from their lows of spring 1926 had turned into a rapid trot and then into a stampede from September 1927. As mentioned in Chapter 3, just as Paul Volcker has been criticized by some for allowing the stock market boom by tolerating rapid money growth in 1985 to 1986, New York Federal Reserve head Benjamin Strong came under fire for allowing the market runup in 1927 to 1928 by acceding to requests from the United Kingdom to facilitate its recent return to the gold standard by keeping interest rates low and credit available in the United States.

(In the first two decades of its existence, the Federal Reserve System was operated in a more decentralized manner that allowed regional governors, particularly from New York, an additional measure of authority vis-à-vis Washington. Strong, in particular, had acquired a substantial international reputation. As Galbraith put it, "Strong's views were regarded . . . with only little less awe than the gold standard."[5])

Strong's defenders pointed to the 20 percent annual rate slump in industrial production over the six months from May 1927 to November 1927 as good reason to ease monetary policy, though a good fraction of this decline could be attributed to Henry Ford's six-month closedown to change over from Model T to Model A production.

---

[4]Much of this section draws heavily on Charles P. Kindleberger, ibid., pp. 77–82 and 108–127, and John Kenneth Galbraith, *The Great Crash* (Boston: Houghton Mifflin, 1961), Chapters 5–8.

[5]Quoted in John Kenneth Galbraith, *The Great Crash*, p. 33.

In any event, stock prices rose by 30 percent for all of 1927 and by another 31 percent in 1928. When Hoover was inaugurated in March, a further 10 percent had been added to share values, as news stories spoke of "cyclonic violence" in the market. Trading volume was growing exponentially, and daily price jumps—mostly up but sometimes downward—were growing larger. Buying on margin was becoming extraordinarily popular, as indicated by the 64 percent increase in broker loan volume from year-end 1927 to year-end 1928; during this time the rate charged for such loans went from 5 percent to 12 percent.

The Strong-Volcker Departure Analogy

Hoover had long been concerned with the explosion of debt in the U.S. economy, though he had softpedalled his views during the campaign. Once in office, he sought, privately, to have the Fed move to rein in the speculative fever with a discount-rate hike. Hoover's capacity for influence with the nation's central bank was likely enhanced by Strong's death, noted in Chapter 3, in October 1928, and his succession by a man much less revered, George Harrison. Strong's demise also allowed the Fed's Washington leadership to reassert its authority in the councils that deliberated on the nation's monetary policy.

Indeed the Fed itself, through its chairman Roy Young, had warned banks in February to curb their brokers' loans and had debated a discount-rate increase proposal. If the immense demand for funds could be restrained, it would also help America's European allies, who were now rapidly losing funds to New York. On February 7, for example, the Bank of England raised its discount rate from 4.5 percent to 5.5 percent to stem the capital outflow.

Arguing against action by the Fed, however, was the difficulty of achieving anything remotely resembling a soft landing. The impact effect of a higher discount rate in the United States would be to draw more funds out of Europe, even if all understood its ultimate objective was to still the demand for brokers' loans. At the same time, in February and March, the stock market had several "mini-breaks" over worries of Fed tightening. As noted in Chapter 3, Charles Mitchell, head of the National City Bank and a director since January 1, 1929, of the New York Fed, took matters into his own hands and effectively torpedoed the Fed's deliberations in late

March concerning raising the discount rate by going public with his own bank's intent to serve as a "lender of last resort," borrowing from the Fed as necessary to bolster the financial system's liquidity and permit the stock market boom to continue. Most thought Mitchell could not have gotten away with such behavior had Strong been alive.

The 1987 counterpart to this episode of Strong's death and the escalation of rhetoric from Washington about fighting inflation was, as remarked earlier, the decision of Paul Volcker not to seek a third term and his replacement by Alan Greenspan. Where Strong and Volcker exercised a measure of restraint over the markets by virtue of their reputation and prestige, Young (now out of Strong's shadow), Harrison, and in our own time, Greenspan had to establish their antispeculation, antiinflation credentials.

Of course, differences in the two episodes still exist. Hoover was concerned about the extraordinary rise in the stock market and the role of debt (i.e., buying on margin), and clearly attempted to influence the Federal Reserve's decision making. There is no evidence that Ronald Reagan has looked upon the stock market boom as anything but unalloyed validation of the economic policies he has pursued for seven years. Further, Greenspan was concerned much more with fighting inflation in the prices for goods and services, not the explosive rise in the price of financial assets. In both situations, however, the lack of reputation of the new kid or kids on the block made the achievement of a soft landing much more difficult.

International Debt and Tariff Problems

While the boil of speculation in the United States was proving too difficult to lance, the Young Plan talks (named for U.S. delegate Owen Young) had gotten under way in Paris to replace the Dawes Plan for the payment of German reparations with a more permanent and realistic schedule. A mid-April impass in the negotiations was rumored to have led France to threaten to withdraw funds from Germany; this breakdown in central bank cooperation naturally unsettled financial markets in Europe, as well as in this country. By June the crisis had passed, and an agreement was signed, but permanent damage had been done to the fabric of international economic policy coordination.

Meanwhile, in the U.S. Congress, Hoover had moved to make good on a campaign pledge to raise tariffs for America's beleaguered farmers by introducing implementing legislation. As is so often the case in such matters, each member of Congress had another constituency that deserved protection at least as much as agriculture. When the Smoot-Hawley tariff bill passed the House of Representatives in May of 1929 and was forwarded to the Senate, its resemblance to a Christmas tree was already striking.

During the summer of 1929, the stock market was *the* topic of conversation. Whether in the market or not (and only about 1.25 percent of the population was in the market at this time), everyone followed its machinations as closely as they followed the baseball pennant races. Being out of touch with the market was to be avoided at all costs, and transoceanic liners were fitted with brokerage offices (in much the same spirit, "beepers" that transmitted stock price movements to investors on the golf course were introduced in the mid-1980s). By the end of August, the market was up nearly 18 percent from year-end 1928 levels.

In Germany, though, the economy was in deep recession, having suffered in less than a year's time labor troubles in the steel industry, a century-record cold snap that lasted three months, and the tightening of credit as funds were withdrawn when the Young Plan talks were in crisis in the spring. The downward-spiraling economy forced the Frankfurt Insurance Company into financial collapse in August, an event that drew notice in London and New York.

The Fed Tightens, and the Market Peaks

On August 9, the Federal Reserve finally moved to raise the discount rate from 5 percent to 6 percent, though industrial production was already on its way down. Historians have made much of the fact that policymakers of the time had a very poor stream of data on which to base their assessments of where the economy stood at a particular point in time, and thus they were more likely to zig when the economic situation called for them to zag. The Gross National Product, for example, had yet to be invented by Simon Kuznets, the Harvard professor who later won a Nobel Prize for his efforts. But these assessments ignore the fact that executives at industrial firms had since the early 1920s regularly exchanged information on the course of activity in their sectors of the economy, and that economic officials in the Federal government had access to these interchanges. Further, even on a modern schedule of data releases, provisional industrial production numbers for July, the first month after the peak, would not have been available until mid-August.

On September 5, in what later came to be termed the "Babson Break," Roger Babson stated at his annual investment outlook conference that "sooner or later a crash is coming, and it may be terrific."[6] Fifteen days later, in London, the Hatry industrial and financial empire collapsed as it tried to borrow several million pounds to facilitate a takeover in the steel industry; when the collateral for the loans was shown to be bogus, trading in Hatry shares was suspended.

The previous day, September 19, proved to be the peak of the 1920s bull market in the United States. In the aftermath, on September 26, the Bank of England raised its discount rate from 5.5 percent to 6.5 percent, as it tried to stem a drain on its gold reserves of 20 percent in four months' time. The French were said to be culprits again, getting even for a perceived slur—and for a documented bold British attempt to get a bigger share of the reparations pie—made by the Chancellor of the Exchequer to the French Minister of Finance during a late-summer review of the Young Plan.

Taking Stock

Breakdowns in international economic policy coordination, a protectionist trade bill under serious consideration in the U.S. Congress, intimations of shaky financial empires and shady dealings, international debt reschedulings, even a stock market guru with a wide national following—many of the same roles in the play of 1987 were represented on the stage in 1929. Again, though, there are differences. Ronald Reagan is long since removed from the nineteenth century tariff tradition of the Republican Party and is very much a free trader (unless one thinks of semiconductors as Reagan's agriculture). Institutional investors are much more important

---

[6]Ibid., p. 89.

in the markets of 1987 than they were in 1929, and buying on margin represents perhaps 10 percent of all transactions, versus 40 percent in 1929.

Probably most fundamentally, in 1987 the last war among countries with well-integrated capital markets was 42 years distant, not 11, and it was followed by the Marshall Plan, not the reparations demanded in the Treaty of Versailles. Both factors suggest a greater willingness among nations to work to harmonize their economic policies than was the case in 1929.

THE FIRST GREAT CRASH

In October 1929, the stock market slid slowly downward. Brokers' loans made by foreigners declined in the month's first week; the Hatry affair and a French desire to repatriate capital have both been suggested as reasons, but a more general one is that interest rates were rising in Europe. The Massachusetts Department of Public Utilities' refusal on October 11 to allow Boston Edison to split its stock four-for-one on the grounds that the company was already overvalued was accorded some role in shaking up investors' ever-optimistic expectations. The market saw the edge of the abyss in Saturday trading October 19, as stocks lost about 3 percent of their value. After mixed days on the following Monday and Tuesday, on Wednesday, October 23, the *New York Times* industrial average fell by 7.5 percent.

Thursday, October 24, has come to be known in the lexicon of Wall Street as "Black Thursday," largely on the basis of trading in the morning, when a tide of selling sent stocks—and stockbrokers perched on window ledges—tumbling. Declines in share prices of 25 percent to 35 percent were not uncommon, and the ticker ran more than an hour late. Stop-loss orders triggered by falling prices accelerated the decline; many of them had been posted by brokers who had received no response to their calls to customers for extra margin. The Chicago exchange closed, as did several others.

At noon, a group of New York bankers met and agreed to stabilize prices, and an orgy of afternoon buying led ostentatiously by NYSE Acting President Richard Whitney succeeded in limiting the day's losses to little more than 3 percent. Volume had been nearly 13 million shares, more than double Monday's 6 million, and had far outstripped all previous records.

On Friday and Saturday, the market appeared to stabilize. President Hoover declared, "the fundamental business of the country, that is, production and distribution of commodities, is on a sound and prosperous basis."[7] But on Monday, October 28, selling pressure struck again, as share prices lost about 12 percent of their value on volume of over 9 million shares. This time even the bankers didn't have enough capital to stabilize the market. With it clear that no "organized support" was to be expected, panic selling hit the exchange on Black Tuesday, October 29. Sixteen million four hundred thousand shares changed hands, and stock prices slumped another 11 percent, despite a modest late rally.

As Figure 7-1 suggests, the Crash of 1929 was immediately followed by a brisk two-day rally; the second day, Thursday, was the first of several days of short hours (sound familiar?) called to catch up on paperwork—and to calm investors. The Exchange closed on Friday and Saturday as well. When it reopened on Monday, November 4, selling pressure remained strong, as it did on Wednesday; Tuesday was election day. After uneven results at week's end, the market slumped further in heavy trading on November 11, 12, and 13. The Dow Jones Industrial Average at that point stood at 198, 48 percent below its level of September 3, the day after Labor Day.

Doing the Right Thing(!)

The conventional wisdom about the Great Depression holds that it was the result of serious monetary, fiscal, and tariff policy mistakes. What is not generally widely appreciated is that in the immediate aftermath of the Crash of 1929, both the Federal Reserve and the administration responded with actions in the right direction, as they did in 1987. On October 31, two days after Black Tuesday, the Fed lowered the discount rate from 6 percent to 5 percent, effective the next day. The regional banks in the Federal Reserve

---

[7]Ibid., p. 111.

System, led by New York, launched an aggressive wave of open-market purchases of bonds to inject liquidity into the banking system.

It must be admitted, however, that the magnitude of the open-market operations undertaken went far beyond the guidelines established by the Federal Reserve Open Market Committee in Washington, which ratified them only after the fact. As noted in Chapter 3, a significant fraction of the Fed's leadership still adhered to the "real bills" doctrine, under which central bank purchases of financial assets not backed by commercial activity (as Treasury bills were not) was thought to be irresponsible (i.e., inflationary). This rigid perspective prevented the Fed from doing all it could as the economic situation deteriorated from mid-1930 onward.

On November 15, the Federal Reserve lowered its discount rate again, to 4.5 percent. Abroad, interest rate reductions also were the order of the day. The Bank of England led the way with three discount rate reductions between October 29 and the end of 1929. The countries of north central Europe followed suit, with each making one or more cuts. Only France and Canada held back, in order to retain capital at home.

Herbert Hoover also moved quickly to offset the weakness in spending thought likely to result from the destruction of stock values. Though the wealth effect had not yet been discovered and Hoover was hardly a disciple of Keynes, the president proposed a one percentage point reduction in both personal and corporate tax rates; for households, the reduction in tax liabilities was between one-half and two-thirds. Although a step in the right direction (America's budget and trade accounts were both in *surplus* in 1929, by a combined amount roughly equal to 2 percent of GNP), Hoover's tax cut proposal could have only a little leverage over the national economy because Federal government tax collections represented such a small part (less than 4 percent) of total economic activity.

1930: STABILIZATION, THEN COLLAPSE

As noted above, the "break" in U.S. share prices had been preceded by tops in several other markets. Still, as Table 7-1 makes

TABLE 7–1
National Stock Market Declines, September 1929 through December 1929
(percent change in national index value)

Belgium	−29%
Canada	−34%
France	−11%
Germany	−14%
Switzerland	−10%
United Kingdom	−16%
United States	−32%

Source: Calculated from data contained in Charles P. Kindleberger, *The World in Depression, 1929–1939* (Berkeley: University of California Press, 1973), pp. 122–123, (c) The Regents of the University of California.

clear, markets on both sides of the Atlantic slumped further in the wake of the Crash of 1929. Nevertheless, the fall in North America was clearly sharper and more abrupt.

As was the case at the beginning of 1988, the American stock market at the start of 1930 moved up. Indeed, as Figure 7–1 indicates, the market rebound after November 13 had already brought the market up about 25 percent from its lows, and it ended 1929 down about 35 percent from the September peak. By April 1930, reflecting a stabilization of industrial production and a slight upturn in employment at the beginning of the year, stock prices were 15 percent above their year-end levels. Foreign stock markets, too, were stable. On May 1, Herbert Hoover stated his conviction that while the country had not finished with its economic difficulties, the worst was past.

In fact, Hoover's comment came at the peak of the U.S. rebound. By June, stock prices had fallen by 16 percent from April levels; by December, the decline from April had grown to 40 percent. Compared with the September 1929 peak, stocks had lost more than half their value. Abroad, in Germany and in France, share prices also fell substantially, by more than 30 percent, between April and December 1930. In the United Kingdom, the reduction in market values was more moderate, a little more than 15 percent.

What Happened?

What happened to make Hoover so wrong? Years of research by economic historians have left us with no shortage of suspects. Nobel laureate W. Arthur Lewis[8] cites the role of the whirlwind of commodity price deflation that began in September 1929, reflecting the liquidation of inventories that had become surplus as a consequence of the slump in business activity already under way and the credit squeeze that accompanied the stock market crash. The Federal Reserve had tried to offset this deflationary impact by lowering the discount rate four more times in the first half of 1930, by one-half point each in February, March, May, and June, but its actions, in retrospect, were clearly insufficient.

Milton Friedman and Anna Schwartz[9] have taken the Fed to task for focusing too much at this time on the historical level of interest rates and too little on the level of rates relative to the investment opportunities that existed. In their view, the central bank should have engaged in preemptive open-market operations to offset the deflationary forces under way in the system. Indeed, in June 1930, the New York Fed's Harrison asked the Federal Reserve Open Market Committee to permit more aggressive open-market operations in Treasury securities but was rebuffed.

Actual money supply levels for September 1930 show a modest, 5 percent decline in nominal money balances in the 13 months from August 1929. More ominous, however, was the 13 percent falloff in monetary velocity (the rate at which money changes hands) between 1929 and 1930, nearly triple the decline then customary for major business downturns. Fearful of the economic outlook, households and businesses had decided to "get liquid," and their decision to hold more of their assets in monetary form but not to spend them slowed the pace of economic activity (recall that a similar phenomenon in 1981 and 1982 made that recession worse than the Fed intended; see Chapter 3).

---

[8]W. A. Lewis, *Economic Survey, 1919–1939* (London: Allen and Unwin, 1949).

[9]Milton Friedman and Anna Jacobson Schwartz, *A Monetary History of the United States, 1867–1960* (Princeton: Princeton University Press, 1963).

Kindleberger opines, however, that since major shifts in the money stock did not occur until early 1931 and since regional financial problems, in the form of bank failures in the Midwest and parts of the Southeast, only became significant in the fall of 1930, there was not a strong case for a different monetary policy until that time. Rather, he focuses on three international factors to explain the quicksand into which the 1930 world economy tumbled. First, international lending, after reviving briefly in the early months of 1930, became almost completely nonexistent thereafter, as falling commodity prices reduced the creditworthiness of borrowers, who then unloaded inventories, which drove prices down further in a vicious cycle. Second, the Smoot-Hawley Tariff Act passed the Senate in March, came out of conference committee in April, and was signed into law in mid-June. It was swiftly met by retaliatory moves from nearly all nations. Though officially the United Kingdom continued to hew to a free-trade line, Keynes, heading a government commission looking into the consequences of the Crash, called for import tariffs and export subsidies.

For Kindleberger, these two developments were harbingers of an international economic system without a leader. The inability or unwillingness or both of London or Washington to mobilize international lending as commodity prices fell month by month implied the lack of an international lender of last resort. The Christmas-tree character of the Smoot-Hawley bill indicated that the Hoover administration had lost control of the legislative process, in much the same fashion described by David Stockman with regard to the Economic Recovery Tax Act of 1981.[10] In England, Keynes' espousal of tariffs had undermined the government's free-trade stance in negotiations within the Commonwealth and on the Continent.

A third major feature of the world economy in 1930, continued economic distress and increased political instability in Germany, cast a further pall over the prospects for international economic cooperation in response to the crisis. Rapidly rising unemployment had triggered central government budget deficits. At the same time, the strictures of the Young Plan and fears of a recurrence of the recent hyperinflation led the new Bruning government to push for the de-

---

[10]David Stockman, *The Triumph of Politics* (New York: Simon and Schuster 1987).

flation of demand and the achievement of a balanced budget. When in mid-June the Reichstag refused to approve Bruning's program, he dissolved the parliamentary body and called new elections for September. In the balloting, the extremes in the German political spectrum gained substantial ground on the center; as a result, foreign capital left the country in droves, and to regain political control Bruning had to adopt a more nationalistic style of governing, the centerpiece of which was opposition to further reparations payments.

1930 and 1988: Trade, Debt, Money, and Prices

The situation in the spring of 1988 certainly bears many resemblances to circumstances in the early months of 1930. The trade bill has been taken out of cold storage, though it has been stripped of its most protectionist features. Still, congressional and presidential campaign rhetoric has continued to focus the electorate's attention on unfair trade practices abroad (this despite several estimates that complete acceptance by the Japanese of all U.S. demands would reduce our bilateral trade imbalance by only 15 percent) and the rising tide of foreign investment in this country.

The increasingly confrontational atmosphere that characterized international debt negotiations in 1987 was only slightly defused by the debt-for-debt swap proposal put forth by J. P. Morgan and the Mexican government at year's end. In this plan, banks would write off half of $20 billion worth of their Mexican loans but be assured of collecting the other half with certainty, since they would be backed by U.S. government obligations. While a useful mechanism for solving part of the global debt problem, such a vehicle requires that a country have sufficient foreign exchange reserves to purchase the U.S. Treasury bonds that are at the heart of the plan; Mexico's reserve position is much stronger than that of Brazil or Argentina. And accounting regulators must address the issue of how it is that debt not involved in such swaps remains on banks' balance sheets at a value nearly double the market value of the debt swapped. Initial results of the swap program have been disappointing.

Debt considerations also have been putting greater pressure on the reported earnings of money center banks. In mid-December, the Bank of Boston boosted its reserves against troubled Latin

American loans to 50 percent; prior to that time, the Citicorp standard of 25 percent, set the previous June, had prevailed. The Bank of Boston action was followed by a series of similar moves by major regional banks around the United States, causing the stronger New York banks to want, for reputational reasons, to follow suit. Not all money center banks, however, have the equity on their balance sheet to take such an initiative. If the Manufacturers Hanover, for example, were to increase its reserves to the 50 percent level, its shareholder equity would be reduced to less than $100 million. To head off such a problem, the Federal Reserve was reported to have requested the stronger money center banks not to "flex their muscles," lest such an action trigger a loss of confidence in their weaker money center sister banks.[11]

Money supply growth also has been somewhat low, at least in the United States; abroad, heavy foreign currency market intervention has boosted the pace of money supply expansion. In the six months to December, both the American narrowly defined money supply (M1, consisting of currency and checkable deposits) and the broader and more widely followed M2 increased at annual rates of only about 3 percent. At the end of January, however, the Fed did ease the monetary reins gradually.

Prices, too, have been generally softer since fall, in contrast with investors' fears about inflation. The producer price index for finished goods declined at an annual rate of 2 percent in 1987's fourth quarter, after rising at a 3.6 percent pace in the year's first nine months; consumer price index changes also have been more subdued despite very strong employment growth.

German Resistance to Compromise

As in 1930, though for different reasons, Germany in 1988 is committed to a macroeconomic policy that emphasizes restraint in demand and seems more internally preoccupied than internationally oriented. On the monetary front, the Germans have shown themselves grudgingly willing to lower interest rates in the wake of the

---

[11]"Fed Urges Caution on Reserves," *New York Times*, (January 22, 1988), p. D1.

Crash. In the fiscal realm, however, German authorities in general and Finance Minister Stoltenberg in particular evidence substantial concern over the federal budget balance, refusing to bring forward all of the tax reductions scheduled for 1990 and expressing dismay at the widening of the budget deficit caused by capital losses on dollar foreign-exchange reserves.

With an inflation rate in 1985 to 1987 of only 1 percent, the German concern with demand stimulus can't be attributed entirely or even substantially to memories of the hyperinflation of the early 1920s. German fiscal policymakers are simply convinced that their economy, despite unemployment above 8 percent (nearer 7 percent on the U.S. definition) and a growth rate slowing to zero as 1987 came to a close, is very close to its capacity and to the "natural" rate of unemployment, that rate at which inflation begins to accelerate. This "capacity pessimism" derives from the official German belief that Europe's economic structures are so rigid, inefficient, and inflexible, and their welfare state mechanisms so generous, that small additions to demand are much more likely to be met by higher prices than by additional production by domestic industry.

Concern over the generosity of welfare-state payments in the context of an aging population also leads German officials to believe that they will be forced to raise payroll taxes or reduce benefits not very many years hence; calculations at the OECD support this concern, concluding that unless such action is taken, Germany's national debt as a fraction of GNP will dwarf that of the United States by the turn of the century (see Figure 7-2). When they know they'll have to tighten fiscal policy later, the Germans reason, why agree to loosen the budgetary purse strings now?

Japan and Other Good News

Several features of the international economy today are much more hopeful than those in 1930. Perhaps most importantly, the Great Depression spawned, in the political realm, a realization of just how dire the consequences of not working together can be, and October 19 served as a useful reminder. In economic life, it triggered a number of institutional changes—deposit insurance, social security, and the notion that government is responsible for herding the economy back toward full employment should it stray unduly—

FIGURE 7–2
Projected Debt to GNP Ratios of Germany, Japan, and the United States

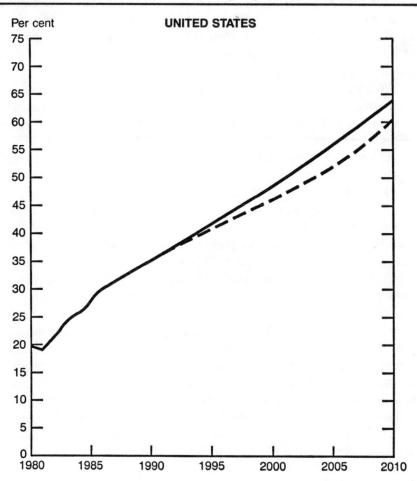

Net debt projections assuming:

__ __ 1. A ratio of non-interest budget balances to GNP
moving towards its mid-cycle value by 1989.

____ 2. As in 1, but with projected pension payment
changes and without any modifications in taxes.

FIGURE 7–2
(Continued)

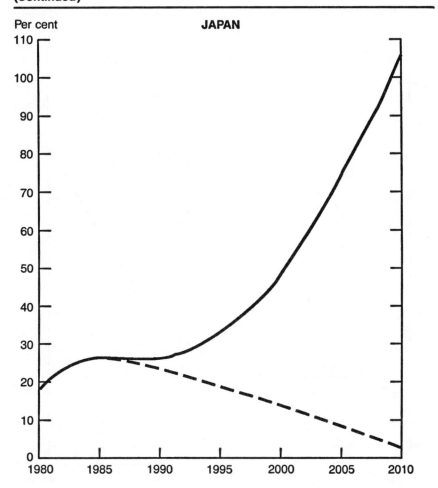

that in and of themselves promote spending behavior by households and firms that will tend to stabilize the system.

Indeed, when the late Arthur Okun found that fluctuations in real GNP in the United States were four times smaller after 1950 than in the first half of the century (two times if the World Wars and the Depression are excluded), he concluded that the reason was the increased size of government. Okun's findings should be

FIGURE 7–2
(Concluded)

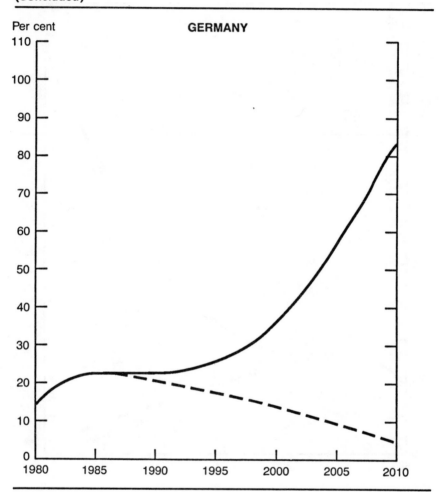

Per cent   GERMANY

Source: *OECD Economic Outlook* 39 (June 1986).

interpreted not in the Keynesian sense that activist fiscal policy had succeeded in stabilizing output, but in the much simpler notion that, with a larger fraction of GNP going to an organization (the government) not subject to the discipline of the marketplace, GNP as a whole would be more stable.[12]

From a more narrow, business cycle perspective, in contrast to Germany, Japan has recorded very encouraging economic growth from the second half of 1987 onward. Domestic demand has smoothly taken up the baton of expansion from the foreign sector as the yen has risen. Government public works initiatives get à bit of the credit, as do relatively low interest rates. Also quite important, however, has been the beginning of what appears to be a structural shift toward a more consumption-oriented household sector. This has been fostered by a recent reduction in tax subsidies for saving, as well as a desire, particularly among younger Japanese, to emulate the lifestyles of their demographic counterparts in the United States and Europe.

As Figure 7–2 makes clear, however, the Japanese face a long-run budgetary prospect similar to that of Germany, and this calls into question how committed their leadership will be to continuing to provide stimulus to the international economy. Though their social security system is much less generous than those of Germany or the United States, their population is aging even more rapidly. Americans (whose reform of the social security tax system in 1983 is responsible for the favorable U.S. profile in Figure 7–2) keep telling the Japanese and the Germans that the GNP projections on which the future debt-to-GNP ratios are based are probably too cautious in the case of their countries. Though the fraction of their population of working age is on the decline, the ability to fund social welfare obligations depends not only on the number of people at work but also on their productivity. In the American view, Germany and Japan can afford to stimulate demand now because in fact they will not have to raise taxes or cut outlays later; their economies will be so wealthy that such measures will not be required.

---

[12]Arthur Okun, "Postwar Macroeconomic Performance," in Martin Feldstein, ed., *The American Economy in Transition* (Chicago: University of Chicago Press and National Bureau of Economic Research, 1980), pp. 162–169.

1931 AND BEYOND

If similarities between 1930 and 1988 give cause for some concern about the ability of the global economy to avoid another Great Depression, it's instructive to examine just how the international economic system unraveled in 1931 and 1932 to see whether any parallels exist with that experience in trends presently unfolding.

As noted, in the fall of 1930, country bank failures began to put pressure on money center banks. The major shock to confidence came on December 11, 1930, when the unfortunately named Bank of the United States, which served the immigrant community and particularly Jewish immigrants in New York City, was allowed to fail. The bank's merger with another, stronger financial institution had been arranged by state and federal banking authorities, but the rescue was aborted after one of the parties, the New York Clearing House, backed out of the scheme, allegedly on anti-Semitic grounds. The bank's failure, because of its name, sent shock waves through the international financial community out of all proportion to its importance to the U.S. financial system. The Federal Reserve did little to rescue the bank or to shore up the system with large-scale open-market operations.[13]

Europe's Financial Collapse

The disease of bank failure was not confined to the United States. Under the influence of deflationary policies in France and Germany, banks there also found themselves in distress; their economic neighbors were not spared the effects of the economic decline under way in the two countries. In the spring of 1931, the Credit-Anstalt in Austria, having been merged with several other financial institutions in distress, needed further assistance from the Austrian government, the central bank, and the Rothschild banking empire. News of the rescue triggered a run on the bank, which turned into a run on the Austrian schilling. Applications to international agencies, in particular the Bank for International Settlements, for an

---

[13]Milton Friedman and Rose Friedman, *Free to Choose* (New York: Harcourt Brace Jovanovich, 1980), p. 81.

emergency line of credit became bogged down in administrative delays; some say the French insistence on Austria's renouncing its newly formed *Zollverein*, or customs union, with Germany was responsible. The Bank of England stepped in with a bridge loan until an international rescue package could be put together; the process took until August.

The concern over Austria's financial system quickly spread to Germany and other neighboring countries. To stem the outflow of reichsmarks, Hoover announced a moratorium on intergovernmental obligations—without consulting the French. Though they stood to lose more than the United States, the French reluctantly went along. Domestic political turmoil within Germany kept the outflows of capital heavy, however, and it took a bank holiday and the agreement of foreign governments to a "standstill" on their trade credits to German banks to quell the capital flight by late July.

By that time, the panic had spread to the pound sterling, as banks from smaller northern European countries without access to their German funds liquidated the British currency to acquire gold. The trickle of funds out of London quickened to a flood, and Britain was forced off the gold standard on September 21. The pound quickly lost 25 percent of its $4.86 value while on the gold standard and in December touched $3.25.

In response to Britain's departure from gold, the Federal Reserve, fearing a run on its reserves by foreign central banks, *raised* its discount rate by a full 2 percentage points in two steps in the first half of October, transmitting further deflationary pressure to an economy already in depression. Later that fall, Britain raised tariffs, giving a further push to the deflationary spiral. In Germany, the priority the Bruning government gave to achieving the end of reparations led it to continue to pursue its policy of restraining demand and promoting deflation.

At the Bottom

By mid-1932, the turmoil in international economic affairs in 1930 and 1931 had produced the most severe economic collapse in anyone's memory. Germany finally had won a financing package that meant, de facto, the end of reparations; by then, however, the

Bruning government had been sacked, to be replaced by fiscal expansionists who were ultimately unable to hold political power against Hitler's appeal. In the United States, congressional pressure had forced the Federal Reserve into massive open-market operations—which it promptly ceased once Congress adjourned. The dollar's connection to gold was effectively terminated in June when the French withdrew all but $10 million in working balances; stocks were 84 percent below their September 1929 peak at the time.

In the United Kingdom, the Bank of England and the government had turned to a program of demand stimulus, which got an additional boost from an improvement in Britain's terms of trade (the ratio of the prices for exports to the prices for imports). Normally, a decline in a currency's value worsens a country's terms of trade because it is specialized (i.e., has more market power) in export markets rather than in imports. Britain, however, was such a major market for other countries that the depreciation of sterling led to an improvement in its terms of trade.

The coda to the economic distress of the period came in the United States, in the long interregnum between Hoover's defeat on November 8 and Roosevelt's installation as president on March 4. Roosevelt's vice-president, John Nance Garner, called for the Reconstruction Finance Corporation (established in December 1931 to provide liquidity to companies and banks in financial trouble) to publish the names of banks who had requested assistance. The banks promptly stopped asking for aid, and the Federal Reserve contributed to a further contraction of money and credit by engaging in open-market sales of government securities. Bank closures, which had begun as early as October and picked up momentum after the election, became even more widespread.

At his inaugural, Roosevelt closed all the banks; shortly thereafter, the dollar's connection with gold was formally severed. At the World Economic Conference in London in June, Roosevelt declined to take the lead in reestablishing an international monetary system based on gold. Commenting on Roosevelt's attempt to manipulate the price of gold before submitting legislation to fix its price at $35 per ounce in February 1934, Kindleberger states: "The Democratic administration was prepared to experiment until it achieved recovery on the home front. It had little interest in or knowledge of the world economy, and lacked confidence in facing it."[14]

FINDING THE PRESSURE POINTS

Is it comprehensible that the United States, Germany, Japan, and the other nations of the Group of Seven could be so irresponsible and nationalistic in the conduct of economic policy as were the U.K., the U.S., France, and Germany in 1931 to 1933? Could the international financial system today acquire the degree of instability that it had in 1931? What are the major pressure points in the global economic system today?

One worrying sign in the international debt picture is the recurrence of what Kindleberger has called the "role of the inconspicuous players."[15] As noted above, Britain was forced off gold when the Belgians, Dutch, Swiss, and Scandinavian banks started converting their sterling balances to gold. The Bank of Boston's decision, noted above, to up its reserves to 50 percent, which was widely emulated by other regional banks, has caused a similar sort of complication for the weaker money center banks. The smaller players, by virtue of their size and resulting temperament, have less responsibility for the financial system as a whole. But acting together, in this case by putting the spotlight on weak money center banks, they can destabilize the system.

What if a run were to develop on one of the more financially strapped money center banks? Federal deposit insurance wouldn't help if the run originated in the fraternity of corporate and intrabank depositors; the Continental Illinois experience told us that. What if the run started on a foreign subsidiary of a weak U.S. money center bank? Who would be the lender of last resort—the Federal Reserve or the central bank in the country of the subsidiary's location? The Basel Concordat, established in 1975 in the wake of the troubles of the Franklin National Bank and Bankhaus Herstatt,

---

[14]Charles P. Kindleberger, *The World in Depression, 1929–39* (Berkeley: University of California Press, 1973), p. 231.

[15]Charles P. Kindleberger, "Depression Ahead?" *Parallels* (New York: Tocqueville Asset Management, December 1986), p. 4.

specifies last-lender responsibilities on a nationality basis, rather than a geographic one. But how well would the Concordat work if two or three banks, of different nationalities and with offices in several national financial centers, all came under attack at once?

Another concern is the excessive reliance on dollar deprecia- tion to rectify national trade imbalances. Again, the observation is Kindleberger's: when the world's reserve currency, sterling, went off gold in 1931, the consequence was deflation for the rest of the world, rather than inflation in the United Kingdom. The reason was that Britain was a major buyer in world commodity markets ("monopsonist" is the technical economic term) and thus could exercise influence on the prices it paid for imports. Today, the dollar is the reserve currency, and the American appetite for imports is well known.

On this reading, the proximate risk of depression lies not in the United States, but rather in Germany, the rest of Europe, and Japan. To be sure, falling import prices will boost the real incomes of these countries. But if their central monetary authorities do not provide sufficient liquidity to their respective economies, the real cost of funds will remain too high to permit these countries to take advantage of this favorable income effect. Realistically, this risk is greater in Europe, particularly in Germany, than it is in Japan. But it must be faced on both the western side of the Pacific and the eastern side of the Atlantic.

How Large a "Wealth Effect"?

As remarked in Chapter 6, the initial response of most business economists when asked to assess the impact of the Crash of 1987 on the U.S. and world economy was to invoke the "wealth effect," in which changes in household net worth trigger changes in con- sumer outlays. Indeed, it is through this effect, as well as through its impact on corporate financing decisions and on consumer con- fidence, that the stock market qualifies as a leading indicator of economic activity. The usual rule of thumb, as noted above, is that a rise of $100 in wealth boosts spending in the current year by $5 to $6. The theoretical rationale is that the adjustment to this in- crease in net worth will occur over a person's lifetime; thus a person with about 20 years left to live would allocate the "windfall" of $100 evenly across time, $5 per year.

Since the original empirical research on the wealth effect was done by M.I.T.'s Franco Modigliani and his associates, life expectancy has lengthened and other factors have been taken into account, suggesting current-year effects a bit smaller, perhaps on the order of $3 per $100 change in wealth. In most research on this phenomenon, it is seen to be symmetric; that is, the impact of a rise in household wealth on spending is about the same, in the opposite direction, as the effect of a fall.

Research on stock market wealth effects in other industrial countries has found them most pronounced and confirmed in the United Kingdom, with evidence less strong on the Continent and in Japan. The impact depends on the proportion of equity issues held by households directly and the size of the stock market relative to the size of the economy in each nation. Stock market valuations are large compared to the economies of the United States, the United Kingdom, and Japan, and in the United States, households own an unusually high fraction of stocks issued. Japanese households' holdings of stocks, in contrast, are relatively low. Hence, the wealth effect of the stock market crash will be largest in the United States, moderate but still significant in the United Kingdom, and rather low in Japan (where the stock market fall itself was more modest). The OECD estimated in November 1987 that the stock market crash would take 1 percent off the growth of real consumer spending in the United States, one-half percent off household outlays in the United Kingdom, and would have a smaller impact in other countries.[16]

Since a relatively small fraction of capital investment financing occurs through new issues, the fall in stock market values is not expected to slow business outlays for plant and equipment much at all. This is particularly true in the United States, where the dollar's decline has increased the momentum of industrial production for export and raised concerns about the adequacy of capacity (and about inflation) in several industries.

---

[16]*OECD Economic Outlook* 42 (December 1987), p. 1.

TABLE 7–2
Post-Crash Economic Outlook, 1988 to 1989

Country	Real GNP Growth 1988	1989	Inflation 1988	1989
United States	2.5	1.7	3.5	3.7
Japan	3.5	3.0	1.0	1.5
Germany	1.5	1.2	1.7	1.7
OECD Europe	1.7	1.5	4.0	3.7
Total OECD	2.2	1.7	3.5	3.5

Source: *OECD Economic Outlook* 42 (December 1987).

To be sure, the reductions in consumer spending are expected to have ripple, or "multiplier," effects within and across countries. Taking these into account, however, as well as the generally easier monetary policies adopted in the wake of the Crash and the U.S. budget summit accord, the OECD concluded that pre-Crash growth prospects in the industrialized nations had been sufficiently healthy that a recession could be avoided. Table 7–2 contains a summary of these projections.

Financial Sector–Real Sector Divorce?

The economic forecasts contained in Table 7–2 seem quite benign in light of the disruption to financial flows that took place in October 1987. On one reading, this is perfectly normal, reflecting the increased insulation from the "real" economy of goods and services production and spending of the "financial" (or as Peter Drucker calls it, the "symbol") network of asset purchases and sales. This "uncoupling" has occurred in the wake of financial deregulation in the economies of the United States and other countries.[17]

In the American context, the two used to be more tightly intertwined by financial regulations promulgated as a consequence of the Depression. Federal Reserve Regulation Q, for example, limited the interest rate that banks and thrift institutions could offer on short-term deposit accounts; because these institutions made

[17]Peter Drucker, "The Changed World Economy," *Foreign Affairs* (Spring 1986), pp. 768–791.

long-term mortgages, they were exposed to interest-rate risk by the mismatch between the maturity of their assets and that of their liabilities. Regulation Q was designed to ensure their profitability and limit their riskiness. However, when market rates of interest rose above Regulation Q ceilings, funds flowed out of thrifts, and mortgage money dried up in a process that came to be called (since the thrifts are financial intermediaries, taking in deposits and loaning them out) "disintermediation." Without the availability of mortgage money, housing starts immediately plunged, and via the standard multiplier process, so did spending elsewhere in the real economy (e.g., on appliances, furnaces, and air conditioners to be installed in the houses to be built). In the economics profession, this tight connection between the financial markets and the real economy was crystallized in the characterization of housing as the "handmaiden" of monetary policy.

After 1978, however, the invention and approval of money market deposit accounts by thrifts allowed them to continue to compete for money even as market rates of interest rose (as they did when inflation accelerated). Housing demand was no longer rationed on the basis of the availability of mortgage funds. Mortgage money was always available, at a price. If the price seemed too steep, lenders were willing (indeed happy, since it relieved them of the interest-rate risk) to issue variable-rate mortgages with discounts on the first-year rate.

The consequence of this change, which was amplified by subsequent full deregulation of interest-rate ceilings and the development of many other new financial instruments, was that interest rates in the 1980s have had to move through much larger swings to slow down or speed up total spending. Hence the notion that movements in real economic activity and movements in financial variables, such as interest rates and exchange rates, have had less and less to do with each other in the 1980s than in earlier decades.

The OECD forecast that seems to reflect this principle, however, is a *conditional* forecast. That is, it is based on several assumptions, two of which are critical. The forecast *assumes* no further large shocks to equity markets and no substantial loss of consumer or business confidence. These two assumptions are closely related and go to the heart of the question over the size of the wealth effect. Upon being told that she had not lost everything in the Crash because it had simply returned her portfolio's value to where it was a few months before, a friend of mine said, "But I lost 12 months of gains in 6 hours."

The essence of the Crash is that it has enhanced the awareness of investors to the vulnerability of their net worth and hence their lifestyles. In so doing, it is likely to reforge the link between financial markets and real economic behavior that was weakened during the recent era of financial deregulation.

Evidence of this increased sensitivity of investors to the vulnerability of their portfolios began accumulating immediately after the Crash and has continued up to the present time. On-the-street interviews of investors conducted during the week of October 19 contained abundant evidence of denial, the first stage of what psychologists have identified as a four-stage process of coping with a major personal loss. People stated that the Crash didn't faze them, that the economy's physical productive assets were intact, that their broker got them out of the market before the crash—anything to distance themselves from the event.

A few weeks later, brokers reported that investors seemed to have progressed fairly quickly through the second phase, appropriately titled "depression," to the third, "anger." Some suggested that the post-Thanksgiving sell-off of stocks was the manifestation of the widespread resentment on the part of investors that their stocks really were worth about one-third less than they had been a month and a half before. Rather than be associated with such "losers," some investors decided to sell them instead and use the losses for tax purposes.

The final phase in the adjustment process is "resolution," which now seems to be well under way. Though the Dow has been marking time near the 2000 level, it did achieve a post-Crash high of 2090 on April 8. Housing starts have suffered large declines, but in recent months have rebounded a bit in response to lower mortgage interest rates. Under the influence of incentive programs, auto sales seem to have held up well. At the same time, consumer and business confidence is uncertain though improving, according to recent polls. Business investment in new capacity, particularly for export, appears to have good momentum. Fourth quarter GNP totals showed a healthy production advance after the Crash, though an uncomfortably large amount seems to have gone into inventory.

The important thing to remember is that consumers remain vulnerable, and individual investors are still skittish. In the same way that the second oil price shock in 1979 brought back all the old fears of the 1973-to-1974 episode and led to lines at gasoline stations, another disruption to the financial system—a second spat between central bankers or a recession-or-debt-crisis-induced collapse of a major financial institution or company (a Texas bank?)—would lead to lines outside brokerage offices as investors try to dump stocks. Psychiatrists say that it takes between one and two years for an individual to adjust to a major personal loss; if a depression in economic activity is avoided in the next two to three years, a major ingredient will be the confidence-bolstering absence of another large shock to the international financial system.

A "Japan Sea" Bubble?

In this vein, another source of potential economic instability is the Japanese stock market, and more broadly the markets for all types of assets in Japan, most particularly real estate. In 1974, the average price-earnings ratio in the stock market was 15; ten years later it was 25. In mid-1987, it had nearly tripled from that level, to 70 (versus Wall Street's pre-Crash level of 17). Even after the Crash, Tokyo P/Es averaged 55, compared with New York's 13.5.

To be sure, this stratospheric level reflects some important differences in accounting and tax practices. Earnings are often understated because of additions to reserves that would be treated as profits in the United States. Consolidation practices also are more casual, with the result that up to 10 percent of income from subsidiaries is ignored. And depreciation provisions are extraordinarily accelerated, which helps cash flow but reduces profits reported to tax authorities.

Even with these adjustments, however, Japanese P/Es are still nearly twice those of U.S. equities, at least on average. The use of averages is a bit misleading, however, since the Japanese market has something of a "two-tier" quality. In part, this is the result of the dominance of the large, internationally known firms in investors' perceptions. It is also the consequence, though, of the much greater reliance on "themes" and sentiment in the marketing of individual securities or industries. While the discipline of security analysis is not unknown in Tokyo, it still takes a back seat to fashion in stock selection by individuals and even many portfolio managers.

Other institutional features also can explain the unusual levels of Japanese securities prices. Large blocks of shares of smaller firms are locked away in the portfolios of larger companies and banks who own shares not primarily for investment purposes but to cement business relationships; some estimates put this total at two-thirds of the total market. Also acting historically to restrict the supply of equities to be traded were the stringent listing requirements in place until early in the 1980s; these have since been relaxed, but the effect on total equity supply is still felt. On the demand side, Japanese individual and institutional investors have been constrained by regulation, custom, or both to confine their focus to the domestic market, promoting wide differentials in P/E comparisons with foreign markets. These barriers, too, are coming down, but the process is not complete.

Economic fundamentals also may account for the high relative valuation placed on Japanese shares. A history of stable fiscal and monetary policy, coupled with an informal corporate-government partnership relationship, has combined to produce a "greenhouse" environment in which companies can take the long view in planning and research so necessary in today's rapidly changing technological environment. It's just conceivable that Japanese stocks are so highly valued because Japanese firms' growth and profitability prospects, relative to those of firms from other countries, are simply superior.

Still, Japanese authorities have been concerned for some time that the historical proclivity of investors to follow the whims of "Stock of the Week" recommendations has gotten out of hand. This speculative surge in stocks has spilled over to, and interacted with, the extraordinary explosion in land values. Urban land prices in early 1987 were over 80 percent above their levels three years earlier, though late in the year a bit of a retrenchment occurred. This surge in land buying has been fueled by banks, eager for earnings as the rise in the yen dampened corporate capital-expansion plans and hence their demand for funds. Estimates put Japanese banks' exposure to the commercial property sector at nearly *seven* times their exposure to Third World debt. When residential and land loans are included, probably one-fourth of banks' loans at year-end 1987 were associated with real estate.

If all this sounds like Florida in 1926, note also that the Bank of Japan and its governor, Satoshi Sumita, have been indirectly advising the banks to curb their lending for real estate speculation and similar investment activities—the same stance taken by the Federal Reserve in the fall of 1928 and the spring of 1929. Rising long-term interest rates in the summer of 1987 also triggered the near-collapse at the beginning of September of Tateho Chemical, which, like other industrial companies having difficult generating operating profits in a high-yen environment, had resorted to *zaitech*—financial engineering—to bolster its earnings profile. Tateho got caught long in government bonds and bond futures when interest rates rose and had to be rescued.

The Bank of Japan performed well, however, in the wake of the October 19 and 20 crash, and indeed the Tokyo stock market, as noted, has held up much better than, for example, Paris, Frankfort, London or New York. As noted earlier, a good bit of the credit goes to the informal discussions between the Ministry of Finance and major securities and other financial firms in the days after the crash. Unlike October 1929 in New York, this exercise in "organized support" in Tokyo in October 1987 worked. Selling has also been modest to date because so many shares are owned for strategic business reasons. Asset allocation regulations on institutional investors also prevented them from putting exceptionally large fractions of their portfolios in stocks as the market rose; life insurance companies, for example, can only hold 30 percent of their assets in equities. Finally, as will be argued in Chapter 8, the different trading regimen on the Tokyo exchange gave investors time to catch their breath and evaluate investment fundamentals more carefully when the market threatened to go into a free-fall.

Does all of this mean that Tokyo's market can't crash, triggering a withdrawal of funds from Wall Street that would make October 19 look like the preliminary to the main event? Certainly Japanese financial authorities are doing all they can to ensure that the current correction in the market goes no further. On January 6, 1988, the Ministry of Finance moved to revive the inflow of funds into *tokkin* accounts, the special investment trusts (total pre-Crash assets, $133 billion) the growth of which had been so instrumental to the market's runup since 1983. In the wake of Tateho Chemical's problems, companies practicing *zaitech* geared back on their activities, and inflows to the *tokkin* accounts slowed. To offset this trend, the Finance Ministry allowed life insurance companies to increase the fraction of their assets invested in *tokkin* funds from 3 percent to 5 percent; since these accounts allow such insurers a way to skirt regulations prohibiting the distribution of capital gains as dividends to policyholders, this additional discretion will certainly be used. On the day of the announcement of this new policy, the Nikkei 225 index rose by nearly 6 percent.

Market watchers still have reason to be nervous about current macroeconomic trends, since a rapidly expanding domestic economy in 1988 is likely to put upward pressure on interest rates in Japan and, in tandem with money supply growth rates bloated by foreign exchange market intervention to support the dollar, could increase central bank worries about inflation. Governor Sumita has been persistent in his public expression of concern on the inflation matter. So far, fortunately, his actions haven't matched his rhetoric and credit has been kept in ample supply.

If any market is likely to expire from the attrition of rising Japanese interest rates, however, it is New York, not Tokyo; higher yields in the Far East would force the Fed to follow suit or suffer another run on the dollar. Perhaps the greater worry in the case of the Japanese stock market is that it will get blindsided by some wildly unanticipated development. Political destabilization in the Pacific would do the trick, but that is a scenario difficult to paint and, on present trends, long in unfolding. The 1920s do, however, suggest another shock to Tokyo's real estate and financial markets: a repeat of the terrible 1923 earthquake and fire in Tokyo, which killed over 100,000; experts say one is due before 1990. The Japanese population is far more concentrated now, and construction works in place are far more elaborate: high-rise buildings, elevated railways, subways, and underground arcades that stretch for a kilometer. If Schumpeter's remark, quoted earlier, about the ground giving way beneath investors' feet came literally true, the loss in value would be considerable, as would the distress to the financial system.

Of course, the source of the next shock to Wall Street does not have to be so indirect. The earthquake could hit Los Angeles instead.

"REAL" VS. "FINANCIAL" PATTERNS

Up to this point, our comparison of the past and the present has emphasized financial factors and instabilities that are either inherent in the international financial system or that could be caused by inappropriate national monetary and fiscal policies. Of course, the ability of Germany, Japan, and the United States to harmonize their policies in this year and beyond will be strongly influenced by the underlying structural evolution of the "real" (i.e., goods-and-services-producing) international economy. Policymakers will unquestionably have to take into account questions of shifting national comparative advantage and the like.

In a similar vein, the length and depth of the Great Depression was affected by more fundamental structural economic forces under way at that time. Some economic historians looking back at the 1929 to 1941 period have placed these "real" structural forces at the forefront of explanations of the Depression; here we assess the impact of such factors then, and now.

The "secular stagnation" hypothesis explains depression by the exhaustion of investment opportunities caused by an interaction of fundamental forces of demographics, waves of innovations and the completion of the exploration of the frontiers of existing technologies.[18] A bunching of capital investment is followed by a dearth of capital formation, with the result that demand in the economy falls far short of production capacity as a result of the classical interaction of spending multiplier and investment "accelerator" forces. A variant of this perspective is the "structural disequilibrium" notion, that excessive investment in certain sectors, or the failure of those sectors to adapt to new competitive realities, is behind the falloff in demand that snowballs into a depression.[19]

A third, but still structural, point of view is one that focuses not on the technological state of production in the economy, but

---

[18]A. H. Hansen's *Full Recovery or Stagnation* (New York: W. W. Norton, 1938) is the leading example of this perspective.

[19]Ingvar Svennilson applied this notion to Europe in *Growth and Stagnation in the European Economy* (Geneva: UN Economic Commission for Europe, 1954).

on the concentration of economic power, as manifested in the distribution of income. In this explanation, destruction of the incomes of the rich in a market crash leads to greatly reduced aggregate spending on goods and services. In essence, "The rich cannot buy great quantities of bread."[20]

A "Real" Story for the 1980s?

All of these theories of depression have some substance in economic reality—that of the present day, as well as of the 1920s and 1930s. The distribution of income in the United States has gotten a bit more skewed in the 1980s, though it's not nearly as distorted as in the 1920s, when it was said that the top 5 percent of the population received one-third of all the personal income; in Japan, too, the current real estate boom has also had the effect of widening what had been a very balanced distribution of income. Some sectors of today's American economy (read steel) have too much capacity, and others (read autos) are trying to catch up with more advanced foreign production methods. And the immediate postwar wave of technological advance may have become a bit spent in the late 1970s and early 1980s.[21] Followers of current market gurus such as Robert Prechter and Ravi Batra will recognize some of these themes in their writings.[22]

The problem with all of these "real" explanations of business cycle depressions, however, is that unless they imply *very* rapid changes in relative prices that trigger a contraction of lending (as Kindleberger suggests occurred for commodities, but not industrial goods, in the fall of 1929, for example), they can't account for the suddenness of the economic decline that we associate with depressions. Because a mature economy's capacity to supply goods and services changes so slowly, only supply disruptions that radically alter the constellation of relative prices (as, for example, after a

---

[20]The quote is from John Kenneth Galbraith, *The Great Crash* (Boston: Houghton Mifflin, 1961), p. 182.

[21]See, for example, the very entertaining piece by Albert T. Sommers, "The (Ugh) Kondratieff Cycle: A Long-Wave Hypothesis for the United States," *The Sommers Letter* (New York: Drexel Burnham, November 8, 1985).

[22]Ravi Batra, *The Great Depression of 1990*, (New York: Simon and Schuster, 1987).

massive oil price increase) can hope to cause the behavior we associate with depressions. If demographic, income distribution, or productivity developments on the supply side of the economy imply a slowdown in the growth of aggregate demand, then explanations of depression must explain why that slowdown was not offset by a reduction in real factor prices or by monetary and/or fiscal policy intervention.

Financial and Macropolicy Accounts

Thus, in my opinion, explanations for the onset of the Great Depression in the 1930s and assessments of the possibilities for a repeat of same in the near future must focus on factors that *disrupt* the ability of the economic system to adapt to the ever present slowdowns in some sectors and accelerations in others. Something must be amiss with the microstructure of the financial system and its ability to continue to provide credit to sectors encountering financial distress, or macroeconomic policy levels must be set at inappropriate levels.

In this genre of explanations is Galbraith's assessment that the Crash of 1929 turned into a depression in part because of the "bad" (i.e., excessively leveraged) corporate structure and the "bad" (i.e., excessively fragmented) banking structure.[23] Almost every account of the Depression mentions the problems with the financial market microstructure as manifested in bank runs and the absence of federal deposit insurance. Out of balance macroeconomic policy accounts of the Depression include Friedman and Schwartz' emphasis of the failure of U.S. monetary authorities; Lionel Robbins' focus on the inappropriate use of the gold standard[24]; Keynes' idea that the problem was incorrect emphasis on deflation to achieve economic equilibrium again at full employment; and Kindleberger's notion that the problem was a vacuum of financial leadership in an international economic community in which the distribution of power was changing.

---

[23]John Kenneth Galbraith, *The Great Crash* (Boston: Houghton Mifflin, 1961), pp. 183–184.

[24]Lionel Robbins, *The Great Depression* (London: Macmillan, 1934).

PLUS ÇA CHANGE . . .?

Which of these interpretations provides the best match with the events of 1987, and what is likely to come after? Or is an entirely new perspective necessary to understand the "market break" of last October and what must be done in response to it?

In this chapter and those that have gone before, we've seen parallels to almost every feature of earlier financial crashes in U.S. and European economic history. Debt has grown to extraordinary proportions, the financial system is shaky, macroeconomic policy mistakes have been made, and coordination has been lacking.

Yet 1988 differs from 1929 or 1907 or 1893 or 1873 in one critical, discrete respect: The technology of the financial system has broadened its scope geographically, and at the same time has bound it more tightly together in time. Computers and telecommunications innovations are *almost* the financial system analogue to the development of nuclear power and nuclear weapons. Just as the latter dictated changes in concepts of national defense, so the former requires modifications in the conduct of national economic policy.

The "revelation" of the 1987 Apocalypse on Wall Street, then, is that the financial genie is indeed out of the bottle. Like the nuclear genie, it can never be completely contained again, but only controlled. We fail to do so at our peril.

CHAPTER 8

DISARMAMENT . . . OR ECONOMIC NUCLEAR WINTER?

As with nuclear technology, we will have to relearn some old lessons and develop some new modes of behavior to realize all of the opportunities for improved resource allocation and greater economic efficiency inherent in the new financial technology, while minimizing the risks of disruption to our economic and financial life. The old precepts come largely in the area of macroeconomic policy, while the new patterns of activity relate principally to the microstructure of the operation of financial markets.

While we're adapting, we'll also have to resist the temptation, enshrined in American political tradition (as it is, I'm told, in apocalyptic theology), to round up—as the police chief in the movie *Casablanca* does—the usual suspects for the market's crash and point the finger of blame.[1] This is not to say that mistakes were not made; they certainly were, as previous chapters have pointed out at some length. But what is to be avoided is a knee-jerk reaction similar to the fairly indiscriminate wave of reregulation of the banking system that occurred in the mid-1930s. To be sure, some greater oversight of securities markets was in order, and deposit insurance was a long overdue innovation. Much of the 1930s legislation, however, simply put the American banking system at a comparative disadvantage vis-à-vis nonbank financial institutions. Indeed, as

---

[1] My thanks to the Rev. Richard Olmsted for this theological observation.

Richard Sylla has observed and as remarked above, much of the energies devoted to financial innovation in the 1970s and 1980s were aimed at circumventing the strictures put in place in the 1930s.[2]

What's needed today in the aftermath of the Crash, as it is in the nuclear disarmament field, is the constructive attitude, in policy-reform discussions within and between nations, that characterizes, as Roger Fisher and William Ury have told us, most successful negotiations.[3] For, if we fail to solve the challenges of the new financial technology, we will be forced to live with its uglier consequences: either a hypervolatile financial environment that prevents, rather than facilitates, the improvements in economic efficiency that are essential to raising the standard of living in the United States and around the world; or an overregulated, inefficient financial system that produces the same disappointing outcome.

FISCAL AND MONETARY POLICY ADJUSTMENTS

In the macroeconomic area, there is fairly strong agreement about what's necessary. About a month after the Crash, 33 economists from 13 countries met under the auspices of the Institute for International Economics (IIE), a private research organization in Washington, to assess the global economic situation and to propose necessary changes in macroeconomic policies. The group divided its recommendations (which were released simultaneously in mid-December in Brussels, Kiel (Germany), London, Paris, Rome, Sao Paulo, Seoul, Tokyo, and several cities in the United States) into three parts: national economic-policy changes; measures to address exchange-rate problems; and suggestions concerning problems in the functional areas of world trade and international debt.[4]

---

[2]Richard Sylla, "Monetary Innovation and Crises in American Economic History," in Paul Wachtel, ed., *Crises in the Economic and Financial Structure* (Lexington, Mass.: D. C. Heath, 1982), pp. 23–40.

[3]Roger Fisher and William Ury, *Getting to Yes* (Boston: Houghton Mifflin, 1981).

[4]Much of this section draws on *Resolving the Global Economic Crisis: After Wall Street* (Washington: Institute for International Economics, December 1987).

Imbalances and Contradictions

The problems in the global economy of 1988, as suggested in earlier chapters, center around the existence of what the IIE Group calls "major and unsustainable imbalances"—the budget and trade deficits of the United States; the current account (merchandise trade, trade in services, and transfers) surpluses of Germany, Japan, Taiwan, and Korea; persistent high unemployment in Europe; and high debt and low growth in the developing world.

Failure to resolve these imbalances risks a serious global recession, or worse. In the United States, this could come about as the steady rise in indebtedness to foreign countries and associated debt-servicing costs outstrip our ability to effect the transfer of real resources—exports of goods and services—necessary to discharge our obligations to foreigners. Improved export capability would then have to come via a further weakening in the dollar; if, as is likely, this were to occur excessively rapidly, it would lead to higher interest rates, weaker bond and equity markets, the withdrawal of foreign capital, and ultimately higher inflation. The surplus countries would feel the reflected effects of more sluggish American economic growth and their own appreciating currencies; exports would decline, and with them, domestic investment. In the developing world, the shrinkage of industrial-country markets (and the protectionist forces that would likely be unleashed) would make the international debt situation even more desperate. This, finally, would reverberate back onto the financial systems of industrial nations, and could trigger bank runs and a downward spiral of reduced spending by households and businesses.

To achieve a $100 to $150 billion correction in the American current account deficit over the next four years—the amount needed to stop the rise in the ratio of foreign debt to U.S. GNP—an improvement in the U.S. trade deficit of $150 to $200 billion would be necessary. That's because debt service on estimated 1990 U.S. external debt of $700 billion will itself be in the tens of billions of dollars.

National Policy Adjustments

Getting there from here, without giving up the gains of the 1980s against inflation, and without triggering a rise in unemployment, will require an artful combination of national economic policy adjustments. In the United States, the growth of domestic spending must be slowed to allow the diversion of production to exports and to reduce the volume of imports. Just as domestic demand grew 1.2 percent per year more rapidly than output in the mid-1980s (the statistical version of America "living beyond our means"), it must grow 1 to 1.5 percent more slowly than production in the next half-decade. While in principle this reduction in spending could come from consumption, investment, or government outlays, the need for promoting U.S. competitiveness dictates leaving investment alone. Thus, some combination of reduced military outlays, lower nondefense purchases, and taxes that lower consumption (but not saving, which is needed to finance investment and exports) are in order.

To avoid weakening a vulnerable post-Crash economy, these tax and spending adjustments should be made, not in the actual federal budget, but rather in the "structural" budget, the budget as it would be if the economy were at "full employment," the lowest unemployment rate consistent with no acceleration in inflation. Most economists agree that the unemployment rates that prevailed around the time of the Crash, in the 6 percent range, are consistent with full employment. And to convince investors that these fiscal policy changes are credible, a multiyear program, legislated in advance, is required. With the structural budget deficit, in the wake of the budget summit accord, at about 4 percent of GNP in fiscal-year 1988, a further 1 percent per year reduction is required, until balance is achieved in fiscal year 1992, one year ahead of the Gramm-Rudman timetable. Enactment of such a program would permit stabilization of the dollar at lower levels of nominal and real interest rates.

In Japan, almost the mirror image of the American policy is required: Domestic demand growth must exceed production growth by 1 to 1.5 percent in order to eliminate that country's nearly $100 billion trade surplus of 1987. (Full elimination is in order because the growing volume of Japan's overseas investments will yield income—exports of services—that will be on the order of $10 to $30 billion by the early 1990s.) This can be achieved by keeping the yen strong and by greater domestic expenditure on infrastructure and consumer goods, including imports. Infrastructure investment can be made by the government, but as noted earlier, the government is concerned about its obligations to an aging population.

A solution to this conundrum is to use microeconomic policies—concerning land-use regulations, consumption-biased and housing-investment-biased tax reform, agricultural price supports, and import regulations—as a complement to the macroeconomic efforts. Research on Japanese saving behavior has shown that, increasingly, it is the high cost of housing that is leading Japanese households to set money aside. Reduced support for agriculture, more liberal land-use rules, a tax code that favors housing as in the United States—all these initiatives could enhance the incentives to increase the supply of housing and to switch national expenditures toward housing.

A similar regimen is in order for Europe and the newly industrializing countries of Asia, though the nature of the directive in Europe's case is more complex. There, much of the current account surplus of Germany has come at the expense of other European nations, reflecting the fact that within the European Monetary System of exchange rates, the Deutschemark has not been allowed to appreciate sufficiently. German fiscal policies need to be relaxed, too, in a fashion that makes a dent in that country's stubbornly high rate of unemployment. An acceleration of the tax cuts scheduled for 1990 would be a natural first move and could be supplemented by a temporary boost in depreciation allowances or by cutting payroll taxes.

It's important to understand that none of these suggested policy changes in Japan, Germany, and the Asian NICs would have a major direct effect on the American current account deficit. Rather, their action would be indirect, via the stimulus on imports of primary products from the developing world and the subsequent expenditure of developing nations on industrial-country, and particularly U.S., exports. Where they would have a direct effect, however, is in the American Congress, by defusing protectionist sentiment.

EXCHANGE RATE ADJUSTMENTS

The above-noted "major imbalances" in trade in need of "resolution" are entirely creatures of the system of nation states that populates the international economy. Similar imbalances appear all the time between regions of these nations (for example, between the "oil patch" and the Northeast in the United States, or between the Maritime Provinces and Ontario in Canada), and yet their resolution doesn't attract such attention or lead to crashes in national stock markets.

The obvious difference, of course, is that the mechanisms available for resolving the imbalances within nations differ from those at hand for adjusting to balance-of-payments disparities between nations. The United States has a single currency, not one for each state, so changing the exchange rate between Massachusetts dollars and Texas dollars is not an adjustment option if Texas is in surplus (for example, because of an oil price increase) and Massachusetts is in deficit. Effectively, the inflow of money to Texas that accompanies the oil price rise will raise Texas incomes and prices; at the same time, Massachusetts real incomes and the prices of goods produced in Massachusetts will fall.

In an idealized economy, richer Texans would import more of the relatively cheaper Massachusetts products, and poorer Massachusetts citizens would import less, until the payments surplus in Texas and the deficit in Massachusetts were eliminated. If this process took too long, two other channels of adjustment would be available. Massachusetts residents could move to Texas, where job opportunities were greater. Or the federal government could take taxes on higher Texas incomes and redistribute them to Massachusetts residents as unemployment compensation. More temporarily, Texans themselves could loan money to Massachusetts.

The Complications of Financial Asset–Driven Trading in Currencies

In an international context, these last two adjustment methods are hardly available. Migration, where permitted, is too slow and small, and—as disputes over the European Economic Community budget attest—fiscal policy in an international setting, in the few places where it even exists, is very difficult to implement. Thus, the choices for permanent adjustment come down to prices and wages, incomes and employment—or exchange rates between national currencies.

In industrial economies, because of the existence of union agreements and other contractual relationships, prices and wages tend to adjust to economic disturbances more slowly than do incomes and employment; both are slower than exchange rates. Income and employment adjustments, however, at least those associated with falling incomes, are the least attractive politically. Hence, exchange rates are looked to even more as the vehicle of choice in international adjustment.

In the simpler international economy of the late nineteenth and early twentieth century, when the bulk of the transactions in a country's balance of payments reflected its imports and exports and most capital flows were either of a very long maturity or involved trade credits, a change in the value of the exchange rate reflected the underlying cost competitiveness of its industries. When a country's currency became more highly valued because its export performance had improved (as the pound sterling did in the wake of North Sea oil discoveries), it served to *switch* the expenditure of the country away from home goods and toward foreign products, thus automatically correcting (i.e., reducing) the trade surplus.

The problem of the 1970s and 1980s is that, while exchange rate movements still switch expenditures from domestic to foreign goods and back (witness the extraordinary increase in imports that accompanied the dollar's rise in value in the early 1980s), the exchange-rate movements themselves no longer reflect only international competitiveness in trade. The extraordinary growth in the technology of finance and the globalization of financial markets has meant that international buying and selling of financial assets, not trade in goods and services, dominates foreign exchange-market transactions. Most estimates put world trade flows in the mid-1980s in the $2.5 to $3 trillion range annually. In contrast, transactions in financial assets are estimated to be, in gross terms, $50 to $100 trillion per year—as much as 30 times greater.

Thus, exchange rates will only *by chance* reflect international differences in production competitiveness for traded goods, and their role in switching expenditure from domestic to foreign goods in current account surplus countries and from foreign to domestic products in deficit countries must be complemented by changes in national fiscal and monetary policies of the sort suggested above: fiscal restraint in the United States and stimulus elsewhere. Indeed, unless national economic policies *are* harmonized, exchange-rate swings will switch national expenditures toward imports in high-interest-rate countries (since their currencies will be strong) and toward exports in low-interest-rate countries, without regard for the cost competitiveness of their producers. These expenditure switches will naturally arouse protectionist sentiment in countries whose producers are hurt by an exchange rate that is too high.

The Unique, Slipping Status of the Dollar

An extra dimension to the current problem with volatile currency rates is the evolving role of the dollar as the centerpiece of the international monetary system. The U.S. currency's lynchpin role in the Bretton Woods Agreement that established the postwar monetary system in 1944, and the breadth and depth of American capital markets, resulted in the establishment of the dollar as the de facto means of payment for transactions in the world economy. In effect, as Charles Kindleberger observed in the mid-1960s, the United States was serving as banker to the international economy because its liabilities were used to settle transactions between countries (and even within many countries, especially those suffering from hyperinflation in local currency prices). For this reason, alone among countries, the United States needed to run modest current account deficits in order to supply the necessary liquidity to the world economy.

The rise in the relative competitiveness of European and Japanese firms since the mid-1960s has raised the mark and the yen to greater prominence in international monetary affairs. Since 1979, the mark has been the centerpiece of the European Monetary System, and both currencies have been increasingly popular as denominations for international bond issues. But the German economy is probably too small for the mark to serve as a full substitute for the dollar as an international currency. The Japanese economy is larger and growing, but until the mid-1980s, Japanese authorities were very reluctant to allow much international use of the yen.

Over the decade of the 1980s and beyond, the yen will continue to supplement the dollar in the international economy, diminishing the need for the United States to run small current account deficits to supply international liquidity. As this substitution proceeds at its uncertain pace, it will remove a source of demand for the dollar and put further pressure on the United States to adjust to its current account deficit.

Taming the Currency Dragon

These currency and capital flows gyrations, and the question about the status of the dollar, would disappear of course if the world had just one currency, or the near-equivalent, a system of fixed exchange rates between currencies. The technical problem with fixed exchange rates, of course, is that the "right" rate—the rate that reflects relative national levels of production competitiveness— changes over time, in ways that are difficult to measure and predict. The political problem with fixed rates, or with an international money for that matter, is that both involve a loss of national sovereignty over the conduct of monetary policy.

Set against these problems, however, is the growing currency, bond and stock market turbulence, and the growth in protectionist sentiment, that infest today's world of floating currencies. Harmonized fiscal and monetary policies can go a long way toward reducing this turbulence, but the current exchange-rate system contains few features—besides stock market crashes—to nudge national economic authorities toward more balanced economic policies. What's needed, to use the language of international finance negotiators, is more *automaticity* in the adjustment to international-payment imbalances.

The editors of the *Economist*, assessing the likely increase in currency market turbulence that will attend the advances in computer and telecommunications technologies that will bind the economies of the world ever closer together, guess that it will take "a few more stockmarket crashes and probably a slump or two" before national political leaders will be willing to face up to the need to subordinate their domestic objectives to the goal of international financial stability.[5] They dub the international currency that will emerge from the ashes of national economic discord the "phoenix," and estimate the time of its arrival on the international scene at 2018, thirty years hence.

If a succession of crashes is to be avoided, more progress than currently likely will have to be made in the international monetary area. The Baker-Lawson proposals for study of an international

---

[5]"Get Ready for the Phoenix," The *Economist* (January 9, 1988), pp. 9–10.

commodity standard, mentioned in Chapter 4, are one example of current thought in the area. John Williamson of the IIE has suggested that countries have exchange rate target zones supplemented with national nominal GNP targets. Whatever the mechanism, it's clear that countries will have to place a *much* higher premium on policy coordination if exchange markets are to return to stability.

TRADE AND DEBT INITIATIVES

Besides avoiding protectionist legislation, what more can be done to keep markets open while the adjustment to international payment imbalances proceeds? The IIE Group suggests four initiatives: rapid progress in the latest in the postwar series of trade liberalization negotiations, the Uruguay Round; strengthening the ability of the General Agreement of Tariffs and Trade (the GATT) to resolve disputes among its members; inclusion of trade in services and agriculture in the GATT or some other framework; and the reform of excessive subsidies of the common agricultural policy of the European Community.

On questions of international debt, increased recycling of the current account surpluses of Japan to developing-country borrowers is an essential ingredient of any solution to the crisis. This recycling is complicated by the fact that much of the surplus accrues to the private sector in Japan. Private or public, however, Japan's institutions are squarely in the seat of the lender of last resort for the international economy today. Japan has the domestic savings and the foreign-exchange earnings; its willingness to deploy them to stabilize the international economy will be central, in the years to come, to our ability to avoid a repeat of the Great Depression

REFORMING FINANCIAL MARKETS
AND INSTRUMENTS

Any student of the politics of the nation state can't be too confident that the harmonization and coordination of economic policy required by the new financial technology will come on stream effortlessly and seamlessly. The *Economist*'s pessimism and the IIE Group's concluding words, "Unless more decisive action is taken to correct existing imbalances at their roots, the next few years could be the most troubled since the early 1930s,'' seem more on the mark than not.

Faced with this nationalistic reluctance to modify countries' economic policies and the international monetary system to contain the forces unleashed by the new financial technology and to thereby realize its promises, two outcomes are possible. We can, in the fashion of the Luddites, smash the machines, segment markets, and consign ourselves to a more modest, if perhaps less risky, rate of expansion of our standard of living. Those who consider some of the new financial instruments simply legalized forms of gambling would have us follow this course, which in analogy goes beyond nuclear disarmament to a destruction of nuclear reactors themselves.

The problem with this approach is that one can't destroy the human intelligence that conceived of the machines, or nuclear power, or the new financial technology. Further, in today's global economy, the only effective repressive measures are those taken in an international setting. If American regulations of the new financial technology are particularly stringent, it will simply be employed in Europe or in Japan, and we will lose its benefits—including the benefit of learning how to cope with its excesses.

The alternative is to try to improve the operation of the markets in which this technology is manifested—that is, to keep nuclear technology, while enhancing reactor safety, all in an environment of nuclear arms control (i.e., coordination of national economic policies).

The Brady Bunch and the Market Mechanism

Fortunately, the gaggle of regulatory bodies that have reported on the Crash of 1987 have largely taken the safety-improvement approach. The CFTC, reflecting the strong influence of the futures industry, has had the lightest hand, finding that the carnage of October 19 and 20 was largely the result of an "unprecedented" shift in investor psychology and recommending that coordination between exchanges be improved. Almost incredibly, the CFTC did not find that portfolio insurance-related trading was particularly destabilizing.

The GAO in contrast, was much more critical of the institutional environment in which the selling pressure was received. It found that repeated computer breakdowns aggravated the panic on

Black Monday and Tuesday, and faulted the SEC for inadequate contingency planning.

The reports of the NYSE and the SEC were quite similar. Both took the point of view that stock price volatility had become excessive, and focused on measures to correct some of the problems that characterized trading on October 19 and 20 and thereby to reduce the amplitude of equity price movements. The SEC proposals, announced during the first week of February, were mostly technical in their character. They included higher and more uniform margins on stocks and stock index futures; the option to settle stock index futures in stocks as well as cash; the adoption of an "uptick" rule for short selling in stock index futures, as currently exists in stocks; the creation of a specialist for the stock index futures contracts on the floor of the NYSE; and the delayed opening of futures markets until the markets in the underlying stocks had themselves opened.

The Presidential Task Force on Market Mechanisms, headed by former New Jersey Senator and investment banker Nicholas Brady, took the broadest perspective of any of the investigative groups. The theme of its findings, released January 8, 1988, to the accompaniment of that 140-point drop in the Dow, was that the securities markets are really "one market," and that any suggestions for improved operations must take this structural feature into account. In this spirit, the Brady Commission proposed umbrella supervision of the stock and futures markets by the Federal Reserve, which would oversee the activities of a still-intact SEC and CFTC; a unified clearing system across markets, to reduce credit risks; more uniform margin requirements on stocks and futures; and—to assist in untangling future market breaks—fuller disclosure of the ultimate beneficial owner in securities trades.

Interestingly, though it found the performance of some market specialists to be "poor by any standard," the commission did not recommend higher capital requirements for them. And it was silent about regulating portfolio insurance, though as noted above, it—like the GAO, the NYSE, and the SEC—identified that portfolio management strategy as a central ingredient in the market's collapse. Nor did Brady have any remedies to offer for questionable judgment, such as the decision on the morning of October 20 of NYSE officials to suspend the operation of the DOT system, thereby breaking the connection between the cash and futures markets.

Perhaps the most controversial recommendation of the Brady Commission was its suggestion to coordinate across markets the operation of so-called "circuit breakers"—price limits, position limits, volume limits, and trading halts. In commenting on the report, Brady went to great length to emphasize that the Task Force did not envision the establishment of new circuit breakers, but only the coordination of existing rules in place.

How Much Regulation?

The art in moving to dampen market fluctuations, of course, is to do so in a way that retains the critical information transmission and resource allocation properties of prices in free markets. The constellation of measures discussed by the Task Force, in analytical terms, amount to the imposition of temporary price floors and ceilings, or their volume equivalents, in the markets for stocks, options, and futures. The problem with interfering with these markets in this way is that the interventions can destroy the liquidity that is essential to their proper functioning. Investor fears of a trading halt, or that a price limit will be hit, can lead them to sell out to avoid being frozen into their position in a security. Like shouting "fire" in a theatre, these measures can lead to a rush to the exits, arbitrarily destroying markets, and investors, in the process.

Still, it's certainly true that a case can be made for interfering with free-market pricing when the prices no longer contain information even remotely related to the underlying fundamentals that in the long run determine goods' and assets' values. This is apt to be the case when prices move very rapidly, as in the hyperinflations of commodity prices so common in Latin American countries. In the hyperdeflation of stock prices on October 19 and 20, the noise-to-signal ratio clearly became unacceptably high.

The Tokyo stock market's practices are often cited as a model in this regard. There are daily limits on the amount by which a stock's price can move up or down, and the limits vary according to the level of the stock's price. The daily bands are fairly wide: 25 percent to 30 percent or so. Further, when there is an excessive (i.e., ten-to-one) imbalance of orders, trading slows down so that there is a minimum time between the execution of orders.This slowdown concept is akin to the "call market" auction process currently practiced on some European stock exchanges. In a call market, stocks are not continuously available for buying and selling. Rather, they are periodically "called" for auctioning. Thus, a given stock may be traded every 20 minutes or so.

All of these devices are intended to give market participants a chance to pause and reflect before pushing ahead with their trades. Rather than being forced to buy simply because everyone else is buying or sell because everyone else is selling, an investor can have more than a split second to assess whether the price moves in a stock are justified by a change in the stock's fundamentals.

What Should Be Done?

Perhaps the most useful suggestion to come from the Brady Bunch and its clones is that the Federal Reserve become more tightly involved in oversight of the nation's securities markets. Despite the central bank's concern over the risk such a role poses to its political independence, the fact remains that nearly six long and perilous hours passed between Alan Greenspan's assurance at 8:15 A.M. on October 20 that the discount window was wide open and the stabilization of trading at 2 P.M. after major banks had been persuaded to extend credit to stock market participants in danger of going under. In London, in contrast, market makers had no such difficulty staying financed during the Crash; the Bank of England and the stock exchange there stayed in continuous contact throughout the ordeal. In a similar spirit, the suggestions for uniform clearing and a clear trail of beneficial ownership are useful reknittings of the current patchwork system.

On margins, the emphasis from the investigators on harmonization also seems to be appropriate.[6] The purposes of the margin requirement on stocks, as envisaged by the Congress when it enacted the Securities Exchange Act in 1934, were twofold: to prevent the diversion of credit from the "productive" economy to the stock market and to inhibit the formation of speculative bubbles in a stock. Though the former was at the forefront of concern in the

---

[6]This paragraph draws on Kenneth D. Garbade, "Federal Reserve Margin Requirements: A Regulatory Initiative to Inhibit Speculative Bubbles," in Paul Wachtel, ed., *Crisis in the Economic and Financial Structure* (Lexington, Mass.: D.C. Heath, 1982), pp. 317–336.

1930s, the latter has been more the focus of Congress and the Federal Reserve since. The empirical evidence on the success of margin requirements in damping down speculation is inconclusive. But as long as the central bank is likely to have to pick up the pieces after a market collapse, there is a basis for requirements of some collateral on both stocks and futures. Any revisions in this area should take into account the differing nature of the instruments; many futures, such as the S&P 500 futures contract, can't be settled in the underlying asset but rather are settled in cash, at least at present. With this minor distinction, however, the basis for harmonizing margin requirements is sound. That may mean lower margins for stocks, higher margins for futures, or some combination of the two. Indeed, in the wake of the Crash, margin requirements on the S&P 500 futures contract have been increased.

Beyond Brady?

As for circuit breakers, NYSE Chairman John Phelan—no doubt trying to get out in front of the regulators—has already announced his intention to consider 10- or 15-minute trading suspensions for individual stocks whose prices move by some large prescribed percentage amount; the CME has already put price limits on the S&P 500 futures contract. Such "time outs"—to cool off the "animal spirits" of investors in the same way that overexcited and disruptive children in a day-care center are calmed down by a short trip to the red chair in the corner—seem worth trying, and are very much in the spirit of current practice on many commodity exchanges. It's true, of course, that a NYSE suspension, if it occurred while trading in London was still open, wouldn't prevent trading in the shares of the many American firms that are listed on the British exchange.

Less wise is the Big Board's voluntary prohibition on the use of the SuperDOT system to execute computer program-based trades to sell baskets of stocks on the cash market if the Dow Jones industrials index moves more than 50 points, up or down, in a single day. Intended to prevent the operation of stock index arbitrage transactions and straight sell programs, the NYSE's initiative was announced (with a 75-point band) by Phelan as a six-day experiment to begin on January 15, the day the November merchandise trade deficit figures were to appear; though the limit was not triggered during this initial period, the voluntary prohibition has been extended indefinitely.

While attractive from a public relations point of view, the NYSE's action flies in the face of the Brady Commission's observation that a similar moratorium on the use of SuperDOT on October 20 actually made the market turmoil worse, since it broke the link between the futures market and the cash market. With futures trading still under way, and portfolio insurers selling heavily, market specialists in stocks were frightened by the "billboard" effect of a plummeting S&P 500 futures index and stopped quoting prices in their securities. At the same time, it's true that if portfolio insurers choose to abandon the futures market and sell stocks directly, that can create chaos on the cash market as well.

But this selling pressure will hit the market whether or not SuperDOT is used, albeit more slowly. The Dow's 64 point rise on April 6 demonstrated this, as program trading continued manually. On balance, the cost of breaking the cash-futures market link seems to outweigh the benefit of slowing down the selling pressure at some prespecified level of the Dow. A better approach would be to make several of the technical changes proposed by the SEC for the S&P 500 index futures contract, while retaining the unfettered use of computer systems at all price levels of the market.

Several other matters seem to be ripe for more action than the Brady Task Force recommended. Principal among these is more capital for market specialists, either directly or on a standby basis via closer Federal Reserve involvement in the operations of the nation's exchanges. (The NYSE on April 7 proposed a sharp increase for its memberships.) However, the specialist system, for all its emphasis on fairness, may be an anachronism, soon be eclipsed by multidealered electronic markets (as already exist in London) and ultimately by fully automated trading systems.

The phenomenon of "cross-market frontrunning," trading in one market on knowledge of imminent events in another, also should be more closely controlled. The Brady Report strongly suggested that some investment banks used the futures market on October 20 to profit from the possession of inside information that selected corporations were going to buy back their shares

The NYSE's April 4 proposal to treat as a violation of its rules futures trading based on knowledge of pending stock trades is a step in the right direction. And it is encouraging that the Big Board will be able to handle 1-billion-share days in 18 month's time. More generally, it is to be hoped that the new interagency Working Group on Financial Markets created by the President in March will actively explore all the pressing regulatory issues—though many fear the group was established just to forestall calls to "do something" about securities markets which remain susceptible to extreme volatility.

WHO'S IN CHARGE?

Macroeconomic policies can be realigned, and financial market structures can be made more flexible. Inevitably, however, something will go wrong, perhaps seriously so. Does the global economy have a lender of last resort, a "hegemonic" leader it can turn to in this situation, as Britain was before the First World War and the United States after the Second?[7]

All eyes are on Japan, but for a variety of reasons, it is unlikely that the Japanese will be quick to pick up the mantle of leadership. Their unfortunate experience with militarism, their strong sense of cultural identity and insularity, the difficulty of exporting their language because of its written complexity—all these give Japan an international outlook totally devoid of the sense of empire that characterized Britain and the United States in their respective heydays.

In this setting, international political relationships could take one of two turns. The Japanese and the Americans could take advantage of the substantial complementarities in their economic and political structures—saver and spender, pacifist and military power—to manage the world economy cooperatively. Or more of a bloc-like international economy could evolve, with Japan the

---

[7]This passage draws substantially on Louis Uchitelle, "When the World Lacks a Leader," *New York Times* (January 31, 1988), Business Section, p. 1.

power in the Pacific, the United States in North America, and Germany in Europe. Neither of these scenarios promises a great deal of stabilitv to the global economy. Japanese and American relationships are already characterized by tension and mutual misunderstanding. A series of economic blocs almost by definition would find more commonality of interests within their membership than among their number. The fundamental problem is that no one nation is responsible for the system as a whole.

SOMEWHERE, OUT THERE . . .

Given this fact, the changed focus and role of institutional investors in securities markets, emphasized in the various investigations of the "Market Break," has ominous implications for further volatility in securities prices. Originally concerned in portfolio selection with individual stocks and stocks in certain industries, institutional portfolio managers are increasingly trading entire batches of stocks at once. These diversified bundles of securities derive their risk largely from so-called "market factors"—movements in interest rates, the dollar's exchange rate, and so forth. Company and industry news is correspondingly less important, while changes in national economic policy are more relevant to investors trading in such a fashion.

This altered focus, made possible by the new instruments and computer-cum-telecommunications technology in financial markets today, clearly raises the premium on international economic policy coordination. Increasingly, the securities markets in New York, Tokyo, London, and Frankfurt will be paying closer and closer attention to the monetary and fiscal policy decisions of national governments.

We can hope that the leaders of industrial-country governments are up to the task in the wake of October 1987 in a way that they were not in the aftermath of October 1929. But the question on everyone's mind, individual and institutional investors alike, remains: Could *It*—an encore of the Crash of 1987, this time almost certainly followed by the Depression of the 1990s—happen again?

Though relations among industrialized nation states in the complex international political nexus of the late twentieth century are much more benign than they were in the crucible of the 1930s, the technology of international capital flows is much more awesome, and patterns of new international political and economic leadership are not well practiced. In the words of NYSE Chairman John Phelan:

> The granddaddy of all granddaddies may still be out there. . . . (The next one could be) 10 times worse than this one. It won't occur for a while. . . . (But) somewhere out in the 1990 to 1992 range, things will really get going again and 1000 points will look like a pretty mild day.[8]

---

[8]Quoted in Philip L. Zweig, "*FW*'s Man of the Year: NYSE Chairman John Phelan," *Financial World* (December 29, 1987), p. 22.

INDEX